Tempus ORAL HISTORY *Series*

Cookham
voices

Fanny Harvey outside Albion Cottages, Cookham Dean, around 1901.

Tempus ORAL HISTORY *Series*

Cookham
voices

Ann Danks and
Chrissy Rosenthal

TEMPUS

Thank you all for opening family albums and sharing pictures, like this one of Jack Brooks Snr feeding his chickens on Sashes Island in 1912.

First published 2002

Tempus Publishing Limited
The Mill, Brimscombe Port,
Stroud, Gloucestershire, GL5 2QG

British Library Cataloguing in Publication Data.
A catalogue record for this book is available from the British Library.

ISBN 0 7524 2656 7

Typesetting and origination by Tempus Publishing Limited
Printed in Great Britain by Midway Colour Print, Wiltshire

Contents

For our families

A classic picture of family life in 1957.

Acknowledgements

We are very much in the debt of the people of Cookham, past and present, who have contributed either memories or photographs to this book. We hope you enjoy the results.

In alphabetical order we must thank:

Rene Allen, John Brooks, Dorothy Campe, Ruth Charlton-Brown, Jill Clarke, Mary Compton, the Cookham Society, John Copping, Tony Deadman, Dora Dyer, Geoffrey Eastop, Pat Eastop, Lucy Edwards, Sydney Edwards, Constance Fenner, Ray Fenner, John Field, Eileen and Leslie Gibbon, Jean Gigg, Pamela Giordani, Enid Grant, Ron Haines, Gordon Harris, Nancy Harvey, Frances Harvey, James Hatch, Barry Hatch, Keith Hatch, Joan Holt, Nancy James, Vivien Jerome, Stanley Jones, Georgina Jones, Pam Knight, Leslie Knight, Ray Lewington, Carolyn Lucas, Reca McGibbon, Esilda Mezulianik, Ray Nash, Faith O'Reilly, Sonia Redway, Peter Remington, Jeanette Roll, Marilyn Rothwell, Eddie Smyth, Joan Stringer, Kate Swan, John Taft, Rick Terry, Margaret Terry, Ralph Thompson, Jack Tomlin, John Tubb, Doreen Tubb, Margaret Tuck, Mable Vevers, Professor W. Vicenti, John Webb, Lynda Whitworth, David Wiggins and Pat Woodbridge. Many thanks to Sue Wilkes for proof reading.

Introduction

When we first decided to compile this book we were lucky in that we had a wonderful and accessible research resource – the people of Cookham. We are both relative newcomers, having collectively lived here for a mere thirty-five years. However we both adopted Cookham as a much-loved home, and chose to bring up our families here. Many of the people who have made contributions can trace their families back for generations. Their grandparents and great-grandparents were farmers, fruit pickers, builders, bakers and butchers. Many of the women came to the village in service to the grand families as cooks or parlour maids, the men as butlers, chauffeurs and gardeners.

There is more than one side to twenty-first-century Cookham. There are now expensive houses, London commuters who don't know their neighbours, country pubs turned into expensive eating houses, bakeries turned into boutiques. However, scratch the surface and you will find many of the 'old' villagers, born and bred in intertwined families. It won't be long before you meet one of the Hatches, Harrises or Tomlins. Ask around and you will bump into someone who remembers Stanley Spencer painting away in the churchyard, or pushing his old pram along the causeway. These are the real people of Cookham. We are very grateful to them all for sharing their memories and photographs with us.

'The Cookhams' refers to three very distinct areas. There's the Village, not spreading very far beyond the High Street, with its sixteenth-century inns and open moor running down to the river Thames. Come up through the Pound and into the Rise and you'll find the station and evidence of the post-war housing boom. It has always been home to a hardworking population. Travel up on the hill and you'll reach the Dean. It has a wild and dangerous past, home to villains and vagabonds, 'civilized' by the building of the church in 1840, and then home to the 'big houses' with their gardeners and chauffeurs.

This book we hope offers you a snapshot of what life has been like in our village. It does not purport to be an accurate history. It reflects what people remember it to have been. Yes, the summers were always longer and the winters had more snow. Yes, people were more friendly and supportive, and neighbours looked out for each other. There was little crime, with doors and houses left unlocked, and the village bobby did know everyone by name. These things are golden memories.

The poverty, deprivation and hardships are remembered too. The camaraderie of the war years, the lack of modern conveniences, buckets for toilets, no running water, families of ten sharing two bedrooms – all these things are recalled, but somehow they all add to the cosiness and comfort of the place we all call home. Some who talked to us still live in the house into which they were born; others have never moved from the spanking new post-war houses.

Many of the memories were recorded sitting in front rooms over a cup of tea. Some came from interviews on our local radio station – Cookham Summer FM. For two years, 1997 and 1999, the whole village participated in running a month-long twenty-four-hour radio station. It was a great example of the community co-operation that runs throughout the village. There are dance clubs, theatre groups, WI's Hospice support groups, a youth club, playgroups, a nursery, both churches have active social groups, and at the time of writing the football and cricket clubs are still surviving. The Day Centre is a lifeline for some of our older residents.

Some organizations are starting to creak. Sadly, Cookham Dean church will be losing its dedicated vicar next year. He will not be replaced. It is getting harder and harder to find willing volunteers to keep many of the village institutions going. The chapter on our internationally famous artist Sir Stanley Spencer comes in part from interviews recorded for the Stanley Spencer Gallery in Cookham High Street. It holds the distinction of being the only gallery in the country devoted to the work of a local artist of such repute, and is run totally by volunteers. Recordings of these interviews can be heard at the gallery.

Our area is so rich in personal history and our interviewees were so enthusiastic that we have collected far more material than can be published here, so the complete work will in the course of time be deposited in our new community centre and library, where we hope it will be enjoyed and read by generations to come. We were not able to include interviews with everyone we wanted to, and we would like to carry on the work beyond the confines of this small book. If anyone wants to contribute then please call us 01628 482715. This will be an ongoing piece of work.

It is so important that the stories and images are not lost. The importance of oral history cannot be overstated. Yes hindsight is a wonderful thing, and memories can change with age, but it will still present the reader with a living history and evoke a time and era in a way a dull official record or report can not possibly do. Where it has been possible we have corroborated stories and facts, but where it has not been possible the reader, like us, will just have to take their word for it!

1 Hearth and Home

Living by the river

Ferry Cottage, where we lived when my father was ferryman, was a two-up two-down place. We had an open kitchen range and no bathroom, you had to use the tin bath in front of the fire. There was a big copper in the scullery and when Mum used to light it up on a Monday morning you couldn't see anything for steam! Originally it was a bungalow, and when my grandfather was the ferryman they brought up four boys and two girls in just two rooms.

John Brooks, born 1923.

On Widbrook Common

I grew up in Widbrook Cottage on the Common. It was inherited from my grandmother. My grandfather was the last farmer at Ovey's Farm, and he died in 1915.

Jack Brooks Snr outside Ferry Cottage c. 1900.

That was George Hatch. Granny Fanny Isobella then moved to Wistaria Cottage, but she also had the freehold of two cottages at Widbrook. My grandfather was a tenant farmer at Ovey's and it was only by chance that I was brought up at Widbrook. Looking at the deeds of the cottage it shows that it was mortgaged about every other year when the harvest was bad and some extra money was needed, and a few hundred pounds would be raised against the cottage. When Grandfather died, fortunately the house was in my grandmother's name, so it must have been a good year then. After Grandfather died Granny wore black until the day she died, which was during the war.

John Field born 1924.

The village green, Cookham Dean

I was born into Royal Cottages, and all the neighbours had lived there for about thirty years. There were the Wilsons who ran the barbers and shop at the end. There were the Appletons next door to the shop. He had been a gardener at a house at the bottom of Winter Hill. No. 3 was the Naudles'. He was the manager of Macfisheries in Maidenhead. No. 4 was the Piercys', a brother and sister and their mother. Bert worked at the brick kiln. We lived at No. 5, and at No. 6 was Miss Webb and her friend. They were very elderly. Quite often one of them would fall over, and there'd be a knock on the wall, and even in the middle of the night we would have to go round and pick them up again! They all had tin roofs, and when it rained it really made a noise.

Ray Lewington, born 1939.

Albion Lane, Cookham Dean

We were brought up in Albion Cottages, Cookham Dean. There were six houses, each with two rooms upstairs, two down. There was a front room and a back room. We didn't say kitchen in those days – just front or back. There was no tap, no sink and no cupboards. In the back room was an old dresser, the copper and a cupboard for the coal. You put your cutlery and crockery wherever you could. We didn't sit in there because it was too small. To do the washing up we had to have a bowl on the table in the front room. There was a fire in the front room, with a little cooker to one side. The well was rainwater, and to get water for cooking or drinking you had to go along the back to the tap. There was one tap for six cottages. When Mother did the washing she had to fill the copper with hot water from the kettle. There was no fire under it. We didn't have a mangle to dry the clothes, so I used to go with my mother each week to this old Mrs House in Noah's Ark Cottages, and I helped her put the sheets through the mangle. Then you'd hang them out in the front garden. We didn't have a back garden, just a yard with an old shed and our outside toilet. In those days there was no toilet paper. We used to cut newspaper in squares and hang it on a string. The dirty water was carried to the drain at the top of the lane. It was outside No. 1, farthest away from the road.

Frances Harvey, born 1918.

Shared baths

Our toilet was very simple – it was a bucket. It was in the toilet outside the house and we would empty it into the garden. You used to have to dig a hole and tip it in. We would have a wash in the kitchen and a bath on Friday nights. The tin bath would go in front of the fire, which was lovely and warm. Frances and I would share it. We would have to be in bed about nine o'clock at night – and

Frances and Nancy Harvey, 1919

I remember leaning out of the window to talk to the girls next door after Mother and Father thought we were asleep. They were quite strict. We would always have to sit at the dinner table until everyone had finished, and I remember on Sundays we would sit and read a book while Father went to bed for a rest and we would have to keep quiet.

Nancy Harvey, born 1916.

Happy with a hard life

Before Mother could have a cup of tea in the morning she would have to come downstairs, do the hearth and grate, lay the fire and light it. The saucepans and kettle were very heavy and black. All of that just to make a cup of tea! We didn't have much but we were happy. In bad weather and the cold the water would run down the walls. You could touch the water it was so damp. My father died in the end, of bronchial pneumonia and pleurisy. My mother had ten shillings a week widow's pension. She had to go to Mr Bayles, the relieving officer in Maidenhead, to borrow the £10 to bury him. Then she had to pay back two shillings a week out of her pension until she had paid the money back.

Frances Harvey, born 1918.

11

Tied cottage in Cookham Dean

I have always lived in Orchard Cottage. It used to be very small. There was no heating except for the range in the front room. It was two rooms downstairs and three rooms upstairs. Two of them were very little. We had no garden, just a fence to the front gate. What is now our garden was all Bramley apple orchards belonging to the Frosts. It was a tied cottage to start with, built as the gardener's and groom's cottage for Orchard Leigh. The tied cottage system was a terrible thing. There was one bad example in Little Mount Cottages. The Frosts owned it but they let it out to the Pursers who farmed up at Woodlands. He was regularly throwing people out, and I can remember seeing someone's furniture all thrown out on to the Common. The Frosts took it away from them in the end.

John Taft, born 1921.

A family arrives in Cookham Dean

My great-grandfather was a gamekeeper, and that was when the Tomlin family first came to the area. He was the gamekeeper for Winter Hill Farm and lived originally on Cockmarsh in a house called Nuttings Farm. My grandfather was the eldest son and he became a painter and decorator. My father was a bricklayer and worked for Hardings, the builder. He worked locally until the war came and then had to go away to build aerodromes. My parents had to leave their house in Bedwins Lane in 1937. It had been rented from old Mrs Baldwin and when she sold up she gave them seven days to get out.

Jack Tomlin, born 1927.

Moved to 'The Grotto'

My grandmother came from Hedsor and was

The Taft family at Orchard Cottage with boys John and Maurice.

about fourteen when she came to live and work in the Jolly Farmer. The floor that she scrubbed is still there! She lived in, and used to do the housework and worked behind the bar. My grandfather was a jobbing gardener. His nickname was 'Tar' Harris, but his name was Albert. My mother was born in 1904, and by this time they were living down Albion Lane in a thatched cottage called 'The Grotto'. That's where I was born. It was very small and there were lots of us. We had lots of sheds in the garden and all sorts of animals, including a pig. There was one oil lamp downstairs in the middle of the table, so if you wanted to do anything everybody crowded round.

Doreen Tubb, born 1926.

Spring water

My father, who lived at Albion Cottages, used to walk up to the spring with a yoke every morning to get fresh water. The men were told they could dig a channel to bring the water into the village so they did – all the way from Spring Lane to outside the church at the top of Albion Road.

Leslie Knight, born 1923.

Born in the Rise

The house I was born into in Graham Road had a coal fire with a hob over it, so you had to stoke the fire up if you wanted to cook. My grandfather used to put kippers on a fork in front of the fire to cook them. It was a lovely smell – and they tasted really nice! I was brought up in Hamfield Cottages in the Rise. They were two-up two-down houses with an outside toilet. They had wells for water – so many houses to a well. It was rainwater, and the men would go and get the water out for washdays and bath days. There were gas-

The spring head on Spring Lane, Cookham Dean.

lights, and Mum had a very nice stove that was a coal fire. My grandfather Hatch had a coal merchant's business. When I was a baby the Great Strike was on, and he used to tell my mother he had to be careful not to be seen taking 'a knob of coal in for the baby'. His yard was at the station, where the houses are now.

Joan Stringer (Hatch), born 1922.

Rain water for washing hair

My gran in Apsley Cottages on Lower Road had a well, and if you wanted to go to the toilet you had to go and get a bucket of water from the well to tip down after you. The toilet was outside and it was really cold in the winter. At Apsley there was one well for five houses, and that collected the rainwater. It would come off the roofs and go through a couple of filters and it was beautiful. We all used to wash our hair with it. We had piped water, but just one tap inside the house.

Ray Fenner, born 1935.

Modern bathroom

When I got married we moved straight into my cottage in Black Butts and I've been here ever since. They were brand new when we moved in and that was in 1932. We were quite modern – we had a bath in the kitchen. It had a big flap on the top that made a good work-bench. When you wanted a bath you put the flap up – and there was the bath. You lit the copper and let the water from the copper run into the bath. We had a kitchen range in the front room and the bath and copper were in the back. I soon got rid of the copper and got a gas one. The copper had a lid on it, and you had to light the coal fire underneath every morning. Outside we had the coal shed, and then the toilet. We had piped water.

Connie Fenner, born 1910.

The village copper

We came to live in the police house in Cookham [now Elizabeth House Day Centre] when I was three. Dad was the village copper until he retired in 1937. He was called back to the police in 1939, because of the war. There were six of us; I had four sisters and a brother. In the police house we had a cell with a big iron gate. My dad was a very keen cricketer, and he used to teach us to play in the exercise yard at the back. It had a very high wall, about fifteen feet, and a concrete floor, so it was ideal to play cricket in. There were two houses with a cell in the middle and a yard at the back. My dad was the Constable, and the Sergeant lived in the other house. I remember Sergeants Tocock, Easton and Holomby.

John Tubb, born 1928.

Gas lights at home on Cookham High Street

I still live in the house on the High Street where I was born. We were a poor family. The people that lived in the village were not well off, just working people. We didn't have the luxuries that the gentry had. We had gas lighting and an open fire, a kitchen range and a copper. Everything was fueled by coal. Mr Hatch would deliver a bag of coal once a fortnight. The gas lighting was very soft, difficult to see with and they were a job to light. The mantle would break very easily. You lit a taper from a match and then had to be very careful. There was no lighting upstairs at all. We got electricity just before the war broke out. We had a tin bath, which you would pull out in front of the kitchen range, and heat the water in the copper. It was hard work. I remember lots of wet washing hanging around in the winter. It all had to be dried indoors, and I remember clothes seemed to be a lot thicker then than they are now.

Nancy James, born 1927.

Living at Strande Castle campsite

My husband and I started our married life in a caravan on 'Ye Olde Strande Castle Camping Ground'. It was 1944 and there were five caravans dotted around the edges of Strande Castle field. To walk from the caravan to the Village we went along a footpath by the side of Strande Water. We were all 'young marrieds' and the husbands were in 'reserved occupations'. There was a water standpipe in the field, so we had water, which we heated on a gas ring supplied by Calor Gas. Heating and lighting were by paraffin. There were however two mains lavatories in a corner of the field. Milk was delivered to the field and we registered for food at Budgens in the High Street. There was a 'Home Laundry' near Cookham Station: sheds with rows and rows of washing lines and flat irons heating up round large black stoves.

Joan Holt, born 1920.

Caravans at the Jolly Farmer

There was a caravan site at the Jolly Farmer for a while. In the 1950s it was difficult to find cheap housing, and the landlord at the time had the idea of using the cherry orchards around the pub for housing. People would take them until they could afford to move on and buy a house.

Ray Lewington, born 1939.

Do-It-Yourself home

We got married in 1947 and we didn't have anywhere to live, so I built a caravan. It was a timber frame with hardboard on the inside and aluminium on the outside. I had a chassis delivered for £100. I built it in an orchard, and of course the trailer went in okay, but by the time I had built it all we had to cut the trees to get it out! Jim Ricketts towed the van up to the Jolly for us with his tractor. We got married in May 1949 and moved in that September. There were seven caravans there, and we paid 7s 6d rent to Mr Yalden at the Jolly Farmer. It was a lovely orchard. We were there for five years. We had a little hut outside with a bucket for the loo and the water came from a tap at the bottom of the field. It was much better than sharing. All our friends when they got married had a front room in their Mum and Dad's house, and at least we were independent.

John and Doreen Tubb,
born 1928 and 1926.

Doreen Tubb outside the home-made caravan.

Mice ate the roof

We moved to the prefabs in 1946. There are bungalows there now (Bridge Avenue). There were just sixteen prefabs in the middle of all the cornfields. They were brand new. They were really lovely. There were four there that were all metal – metal cupboards – and the other twelve were all wood. We were the second to move in next to Mrs Robinson. They were really smashing. The fire heated all the room and you had everything laid on; fridge, electric stove, electric copper. We had two double bedrooms and a sitting room and a nice big kitchen, and a bathroom and loo, and a good-sized garden. The prefabs were warm and cosy. We used to get mice as lodgers. They used to eat the ceiling. They'd chew it right down to a very thin layer so that if you touched it your finger went through. While we were living there they built the rest of the council estate around us. The prefabs came down in 1978. They were up for thirty-two years – they were only supposed to be up for ten!

Lucy and Sydney Edwards,
born 1914 and 1918.

Leaky roof

After my husband died, my son and I left Rowborough and after a few moves I bought a little house, one of the Nissan huts that were down in Hillyers Dell, one of the prefabs. The house was called Hillyers Dell, Hillyers was on the corner. It leaked like a sieve. The tiles on the roof had no lining so whenever we had a rainstorm I had to leap up in to the attic. I got the idea of putting up long cloths to control the dripping, so the water would run down to the floor. That only really lasted for a year or so, but I managed to sell it for more than I paid, leaks and all, and moved on.

Vivien Jerome (Mrs Ripley), born 1909.

Sent to Cookham Dean

My grandfather built the church in Cookham Dean. John Knight was a stonemason and

Vivien Ripley sits with a friend outside Hillyers Dell.

originally came to Cookham to repair the church tower at Holy Trinity. He met a lady in the Village – Mrs Knib. She'd been widowed and had about fourteen children. They moved in together but the church elders said they shouldn't be allowed to live together [without being married]. They sent her up to Cookham Dean – where all the baddies were sent in those days. So my grandmother ended up living in Albion Cottages where they had two bedrooms for all those children. My grandfather followed her up to the Dean. He walked all the way to Reading to get a vicar to come and marry them because he didn't want the one from down in Cookham who had turned her out of the Village – and they were married on the green outside where Cookham Dean church is now. They then had two more children – one of whom was my father, Frederick.

Leslie Knight, born 1923.

High living

In 1932 my mother, Marjorie Castellanos, was looking for a suitable place to have a house built and she was brought up to this hill where there were just fields. It was orchard all the way from Lea Barn to Dean Lane. She was offered the house next door, which was nearly built, but it had no view. It was raining hard and was so misty that she thought it was like being by the sea. She said, 'if I can buy this piece of land I'll have a house here'. Before the war my mother had help in the house – in fact she had rather a lot of help for this house, as there were only the two of us living in it. There was a man who came in to stoke the boilers in the morning, a cook who lived in the village at the bottom of Startins Lane, a housemaid/nurse for me, somebody who came a couple of times a week to do the rough work, and a gardener one day a week.

Esilda Mezulianik (Castellanos), born 1929

Tales of the river

When my husband Geoffrey came to work at the pottery at Odney in 1953 we lived on a houseboat. The boat was very, very tiny, with bunks and a small galley with a table, chairs and a cooker. We started living there in the spring and the lovely thing was you saw the spring coming out of the ground because you were so close to the bank. All the marvellous life of the riverbank was literally under your nose. We had a lovely party once, with a bonfire on the island we were moored up against, and some people dived for knives and forks we had dropped in the water. Geoffrey had to row across the river every morning to get to work.

Pat Eastop

Costly rental

My grandfather left me Slate Cottage, which is at the top of Kings Lane in Cookham Dean. I sold it in 1963 when I realized it was costing me money. It had a sitting tenant at 5s 11d a week. It was a controlled rent and I couldn't do anything about it. It was costing so much to maintain that I just had to sell it for £750.

Pat Woodbridge, born 1927.

Weekend cottage

We first came to Cookham in 1932. We lived in Hampstead during the week and we took on the property next to the Kings Arms as a weekend cottage. We would come down on a Friday evening and I would have to go back on a Sunday afternoon to be ready for school. Mummy came up later with the maid and Daddy went up on the early train to the office. Later when Daddy became ill we moved to Cookham permanently.

Pam Giordani, born 1920.

Esilda Castellanos in the orchards by her new home.

Cookham village.

New home needed

In 1936 Mr Lawrence, the landlord who lived at Dyers, came to the six residents of Albion Cottages, Cookham Dean, and told us they were unfit for human habitation, that we must find other accommodation and that he was to demolish them. It nearly broke my mother's heart. She had lived with her parents in that cottage. As you know they stand to this day. The rent was 3s 9d – out of my mother's ten shillings pension. She had 6s 3d left to keep the three of us on, Mother, me and my sister Nancy. Later in 1937 we moved into Sleekstone Cottages, Grange Road, when they were brand new. There was nothing else around apart from the post office; it was just cabbage fields.

Frances Harvey, born 1918.

Building begins

Directly after the war lots of houses were built. We had lots of evacuees and new people and the new estates were built. Coxborrow Close, Burnt Oak and Westwood Green were all farmland before. The houses were in the middle bit. It was always the rich, – the middle and the rich. This bit [Cookham Rise] was the poor common bit. There's still that divide now. There's money up the Dean and in the Village. It has levelled itself out from what it used to be.

Jeanette Roll (Edwards), born 1941.

Stayed put

We moved to Hillcrest Avenue when the house was brand new, and I've lived here fifty years. There were a couple of big houses in Lyndhurst Avenue, but most of the area was allotments and cornfields. We would watch the partridges walk through the corn. The recreation ground was quite overgrown. It was cut once or twice a year for hay, and the top part was cut for the football field and

Westwood Green fifty years on.

there were allotments. When we moved in we had two bedrooms and a kitchen and an indoor bathroom. It was very nice. My grandfather had an allotment on Lower Road, and I can remember the houses being built along there. People would buy a plot and have a house built, one at a time.

Joan Stringer (Hatch), born 1922

Coxborrow was brand new

My first sight of Cookham was from the railway station. I had heard there were some houses being built and a friend of mine had bought one, although I didn't know Cookham at all. I arrived at the station with my young daughter and walked up and there was a little shop – dear Mrs Swatton's – and I said 'Coxborrow?' and she said 'just up there'. It was very barren. There were some houses built, and there was one with just a foot-board to get into the front door. There were no workmen around at all. The next door one

was occupied, so I went in and saw it and thought it would be home. There were stairs straight up, three bedrooms, inside bathroom, a lounge and dining room combined. What more could you want? I'd come from Leeds and I thought Cookham was a very tiny, isolated place. We paid £2450 in 1954.

Dorothy Campe, born 1913.

Welcome home

We came on to Westwood Green when it had been built for about five years. People were still a bit resentful that the beautiful orchards had gone. There's a wonderful spirit round here. We did move out for a while, and went to live in Sutton Road. We came back in 1988, and we had thirty-two cards from neighbours saying 'welcome back'.

Rick Terry.

2 Going to School

Holy Trinity School

I went to Holy Trinity in the early 1930s. I lived at The Gate public house and walked down through the Pound, across the Moor and into school four times a day. Lunchtime was two hours and all the children walked home, some far further than I did. The school at that time was just the old red-brick buildings. The outside building was the infants', and the inside building had two rooms in which there was the mixed first and second year juniors. Mrs Adams' room, which was the third and fourth year juniors, was partitioned off. The Revd Hayward Browne used to come in three times a week and we would chant the creed and commandments and learn chunks out of the Bible.

Lynda Whitworth (Pat Thompson), born 1925.

Daydreaming

I remember an eclipse of the sun while I was at Holy Trinity school. I was a monitor and I was going to take the registers out to the little

Holy Trinity School band c. 1930.

classes and I remember feeling all creepy. Very odd, I can recall that very plainly. I remember sitting and dreaming through something or another and then I made a mistake because I had written something in a book and I'd torn a page out, and I was made to stand on the form every playtime for a week for that misdemeanour. I got told off for talking to the boys. They were segregated from the girls at playtime and in the classroom and I was caught talking, to one of the Purser boys, I think it was.

Kate Swan, born 1911.

Lunch with Granny

I can't honestly say I enjoyed school – it was much better to be out of it. I remember the size of the rooms when I got there. Our cottage at Widbrook was very small, with low ceilings and Holy Trinity seemed vast to me. Sometimes Granny Fanny Hatch would meet me for lunch or I would go round to Wistaria Cottage after school by way of the High Street. I'd stop at the forge and watch the horses being shod. The horses were very patient as they had those hot shoes fitted and I can still remember the smell.

John Field, born 1924

Grandmother Fanny Isobella Hatch.

four or five. He never said what he'd done. If you didn't have anything to do they would give you a piece of cloth and you had to do fraying, fraying… it was the most boring thing!

Margaret Tuck, born 1937.

Strict discipline

I started in 1942. We had one really strict teacher – Mrs Snapes! You did learn with her though… She had grey hair in a bun. I don't ever remember her having a book with her to teach us. I suppose she'd done it for so long she just remembered. She taught my mother-in-law, Alice Turner from Widbrook, and my dad, Percy. She retired towards the end of the 1940s. Mr Snapes used to sing in the choir at the church. My dad said he got the cane the first day he went to Holy Trinity, aged about

Boys were 'grubs'

Mrs Snapes had steel blue eyes and thick glasses, which made her eyes look twice as big as normal, and her stare would rivet you to the ground. She didn't even have to lift a finger! She referred to boys as 'horrid little grubs'. Mrs Stanton came in as a supplementary teacher during the war. Mr and Mrs Stanton lived in a tin-clad shed in the garden behind the Kings Arms. In 1936, Pinder Hall opened and at Christmas Holy Trinity school put on a show. The senior school, Mrs

A class at Holy Trinity School, 1931.

Adams' and Mrs Snapes' classes, put on Snow White and the Seven Dwarfs. I played a nursery rhyme part and was the dish that ran away with the spoon! The school day would start at nine with morning prayers, which would be followed by a half an hour scripture lesson. Then it would be the three Rs – always arithmetic, always composition and always reading. When your joined up handwriting was ready you used pen and ink. We had PE twice a week, when all classes would go into the girls' playground at the back of the school. The boys used to play in the front – there was segregation from the age of seven. In the afternoon we would have history, geography and at least one more period of arithmetic. On Fridays in Mrs Snape's class we would do 'silent reading' while the teachers wrote their weekly reports. Then once she had done her work she would read to us.

James Hatch, born 1930.

Dancing round the maypole

I remember the headmistress was Mrs Adams, and before that Mrs Brown. The head used to live in the house at the side, which was then taken over for the verger to live in. We always went to Mellmott Lodge to dance round the Maypole on the first of May. It had a lovely garden. We only ever seemed to have thin white dresses on – no cardigans, so the weather must have been better!

Joan Stringer, born 1922.

Singing games

I started to teach at Holy Trinity in 1955, and every May we'd have dancing round the maypole, and a Queen. She had a pretty dress. The children would learn maypole dancing. There were about 100 children, and in the playground they would play singing games. They would play 'In and Out the Windows' and 'I Sent a Letter to My Love' – really simple games. They didn't play with balls, and there was no football because there wasn't room. It was all very sedate and gentle. School dinners were mostly mince and potato, spotted dick and custard or semolina pudding. I retired in 1978. The new houses that had been built meant there were lots more children in the village. They all had a desk, but it was very squashed. As the numbers increased they built the new hall at the side of the school. In those days though children were obedient. They would, on the whole, do what you asked them to do. The main punishment was to keep them in at break times! There was the cane when I first arrived, but we soon dropped that.

Georgina Jones, born 1917.

Warm milk

I had a slate the first time I went to school. I was not quite five and I was allowed to sit with my friend. We didn't wear uniforms, and would come home for lunch. We used to have milk, which I hated. They used to put it on the combustion stove and they would put the crate of milk on there in the morning to warm for us. The two classes were divided with a sliding door and at Christmas when we had school parties they would slide it open. When we were in the third year at Holy Trinity we made pyjamas and a nightdress all by hand, which were then given to the children's ward at Maidenhead Hospital. Our teachers were very strict. You used to get the ruler very often across your knuckles for talking or playing around. The boys used to get the cane on the hand. Mrs Snapes would often hit us. We used to have PE out in the playground. They called it 'drill' and we

Maypole dancing at Holy Trinity c. 1953.

made mats for ourselves out of thick paper card, which we had to buttonhole all the way round. We would do PE in the winter when it was very cold in shorts and a top. We had scripture every day, reading from the bible, and the vicar Hayward Browne used to come on a Friday.

Nancy James, born 1927.

Dad was headmaster

I was six when I came to Cookham. My father, Haydn Jenkins, became the headmaster of Holy Trinity school in 1949 and we came to live in the little house attached to the school. One of the first things he did was to reinstate the use of the school bell. I think he bought a new bell rope, and I remember it hung down in the large classroom at the front of the school. He would ring the bell every morning at 8.45 and you could hear it all over the village. School lunches were delivered in metal containers and we would get a small roll of oilcloth out of our desks and have lunch sitting at them. My father would serve the meal from the containers on trestle tables. We had milk at morning break. The milk monitor would bring the milk from the small front porch where we hung our coats. The bottles had cardboard tops with a pre-formed hole in, which was punched out for the straw to fit through. We would make mats out of the tops in our art classes. In the winter the milk would be frozen. Sometimes my mother would heat the milk on the stove and add cocoa powder. What luxury…

Enid Grant (Jenkins), born 1943

Tin cup on a string

In the infants our toilets were in a tin lean-to on the edge of the building and in there were three hand basins and lumps of carbolic soap. On a wet day we'd hang our coats in there and the smell was disgusting. There was a tin cup in there on a piece of string if we wanted a drink of water. We had milk in the mornings, which would come from White Place Farm, courtesy of Lady Astor. The price was one halfpenny a day. You took twopence halfpenny on a Monday morning and gave it to the teacher. That was your milk money for the week.

James Hatch, born 1930.

White Place Farm milk bottle top.

Cookham Dean School

I started in the nfants at Cookham Dean in the old building, which is still used. When we were a bit older we went to the junior mixed school, which was in the building behind what was the garage. Miss Sally Lomas was the headmistress. When I was at the infants I loved to go outside, because there were harebells growing in the grass by the side of the school. I do remember them and they were lovely.

Frances Harvey, born 1918.

Cookham Dean headmaster Mr Edwards with the local football team, 1904.

Forgot pinafore

I was very nervous and cried one day when I got to school and realized I'd left my pinafore at home. We used to wear pinafores with a little frill round. They were very comfortable and I was lost without it. We used to have to wear gymslips, black stockings and black boots with laces. We hated those boots. The boys wore grey jackets and trousers. One year we put on a play – 'The Maid of the Mountains' – I was very nervous, always wanting to be at the back of the stage. We did it in the hall and all the parents came.

Nancy Harvey, born 1916.

Ran away on the first day

I remember I ran home twice on my first day at school. Miss Gosling came and got me on the Common the first time and the second time my mother chased me back with a stick! Because we lived next to Cookham Dean school I can just about remember Mr Edwards, although he had left school a long time before I went there. I had Miss Lomas. She was terrifying. I can always remember her flogging a young girl and that has stuck in my memory. She came from Cookham Rise and had done her sums wrong or something, and she got the cane in front of the class. You went to the main building from five to seven years old, and then from seven to eleven you went to the school down the road in School Lane. From eleven to fourteen I went to Cookham Rise Senior school. Miss Lomas was at the middle school. Miss Gosling took the infants and she was very nice

John Taft, born 1921.

School became a garage

I started at Cookham Dean in 1932 and saw the end of the old school [in School Lane] We would go down there for the odd lesson. It was two rooms – one on the left and one on the right. It must have closed fairly soon after that because I only remember that in the very early days. Then it was turned into a garage. You didn't see many cars in those days – we'd play football all the way up to school in the road. Most of the larger houses had a car and they were maintained there.

Pat Woodbridge, born 1927.

Not wanted

I went to school at Cookham Dean, although I wasn't wanted because it was a church school and we weren't in the parish. Hockett Lane was in the parish of Bisham. The old school at Cookham Dean was converted into a garage in the 1930s. The stucco frieze at the top was done by a Cookham Dean man, Jim Grainger. He was a plasterer by profession.

Ray Nash, born 1929.

Empire Day celebrations

Miss Lomas shouted at me the first day 'Don't run down the corridor. My children do not run'. There was a long corridor with a dark red door, which had a huge knob in the middle. It was so big that no child could have opened it. This was the building in School Lane. We went from there up to the main school where Mrs H.K. Lewis was the head teacher. We would always celebrate Empire Day at Cookham Dean. The Union Jack would be flying and we'd all sing. It was a big day. We'd dance round the maypole, boys and girls. You'd weave in and out making

Outside the old Cookham Dean school building in the early 1930s.

Mrs Lewis and her class in the 1940s.

patterns. We were brought up to believe that the flag was very special. We always had one at home. I got the 'never absent, never late' prize at Cookham Rise Senior school!

Doreen Tubb, born 1926.

Hated Horlicks

We had a teacher called Mrs Lewis and she was a Welsh tyrant. She'd walk round with the cane and rap your knuckles. Miss Keeling was a local teacher and she was very kind. We used to have Horlicks, which was introduced during the thirties. I used to hate it. Everyone went home for lunch from 12 till 1.20 p.m. We'd finish at about three o'clock. I enjoyed my schooldays.

Pat Woodbridge, born 1927.

First day treat

I started in 1937. I can remember on the first

day walking up Chalk Pit Hill from Kings Lane, crying my eyes out. The school day I can't remember but I do remember running back to my father on the farm at the end of the day and getting on the old horse and van which they used to get the fruit in from the orchards. We went and collected some apples ready to go to London. I can remember my father letting me drive the horse that day because I'd been a good boy at school.

Gordon Harris, born 1932.

On to Cookham Rise Secondary School

Bill Turner was my headmaster at Cookham Dean, and he was very keen on sport. I used to play a lot of cricket on the common outside the school. We used to have fairs and the school fête in the grounds of Dean House on the Cricket Common. There was a grass tennis court in Dean House gardens, and that's where we would have the Cookham

Dean school fête. We would have stalls and flags everywhere. I went down to Cookham Rise Secondary school, with 'Gaffer' Woods as my teacher. Mr Griffiths was the sports master, and we did a lot of athletics. We entered for County Championships.

Ray Lewington, born 1939.

School allotments

Cookham Rise Secondary was a marvellous school. We had a good headmaster down there, George Woods, but we didn't have many teachers because it was wartime. I remember Miss Graham was the other teacher. We had a big allotment in what is now the Alfred Major Playing Fields that belonged to the school. We used to enjoy ourselves working on the allotment. We would bring all the stuff up, cabbages and carrots, and the school used to sell it.

Raymond Nash, born 1929.

Digging in rhythm

We used to go to the allotment after school. I remember the first dig we had – Gaffer Woods had us all in one line. We each had a spade and we dug to a rhythm. It was to teach us gardening and the produce was sold for the school funds. We grew mostly vegetables.

Pat Woodbridge, born 1927.

Got the cane

I got the cane at Cookham Rise two or three times. We had a Mr Hutchins, who caned me once because I was talking in class. I had to stand up on the seat and repeat some lines, and then he caned my hand. I told my mother when I got home and she said, 'I expect you deserved it!' We used to play netball and I went to the county sports meeting at Wargrave. I used to do hurdling and high jump.

Nancy Harvey, born 1918.

Cookham Rise class of '48.

Mr Hutchins leads a Cookham Rise School outing.

Saved by sport

I was only interested in football at school. I went to Cookham Rise Senior school and left at fourteen. I didn't like school much. We had a horrible schoolmaster, Mr Hutchins. He was alright to me, I think because I liked football. He had a cane, and would flog boys in front of the class.

John Taft, born 1921.

Won lots of prizes

Cookham Rise Secondary school was a happy school, but it had no mod cons. The toilets were nothing but buckets, which the caretaker had to see to. I loved school and I won a lot of prizes. I got a medal that was given by the War Memorial Committee for most popular pupil. There were two, a silver and a bronze. I got the bronze. I suppose they did it to encourage the pupils.

Joan Stringer, born 1922

Not allowed to mix

I went to kindergarten in Maidenhead, and then I had a home tutor for while. I then went to Maidenhead College, then had another home tutor. I didn't go to the local village school because of the social structure that existed in the village at the time. I wasn't allowed to mix with the local children. I then went to Sir William Borlase

Frances Harvey in her County Girls' uniform c. 1931.

school, in Marlow. It was just at the time when it was still a private school, with boarders with the Revd Skinner.

Peter Remington, born 1922.

Changes to a primary school

In the early 1960s I returned to Cookham as a qualified, experienced teacher, and taught English for one term at Cookham Rise Secondary school with my old headmaster Mr Wood as my boss! The school then became a primary school, and Mr Wood and I had the task of starting a school – buying all the books, materials etc. Ivor Sayer became headmaster after Mr Wood died. We had a lot of building done; the hall had to be extended. Mrs Waite had to cook all the dinners there, so we had a kitchen put in. Later we had some playground apparatus put in and the newly formed PTA raised funds to have a swimming pool installed.

Lynda Whitworth, born 1925.

Scholarship caused problems

I won the Berkshire scholarship from Cookham Rise Secondary Council school. It only covered tuition at the county girls school, not uniform, travel or books – my poor mother, she went out scrubbing floors otherwise I couldn't have stayed at the school.

Frances Harvey, born 1918.

3 Cookham Village Life

The Village was lovely

We first arrived in the village in 1959. I didn't know a soul. My husband Tom would come home from London in the evening and say did you meet anyone? and I'd say yes, I met the postman and the grocer and the milkman. But eventually I met lots of people. The High Street was full of life. The tradespeople were all there, you see. They're not there now. There was the butcher, the baker, the post office, the greengrocers – there was everything. Jack Smith, the butcher, was full of fun. The International Stores was further up the High Street, and if ever I was in difficulty Jack would ring to see if I needed anything. Then I would ring the grocer to deliver some stuff and the two would liaise, and my groceries and meat would arrive at the same time. It was lovely.

Ruth Charlton Brown, born 1916.

Visits

When we first moved into the village we had visits from tradesmen within days of moving in. We had Mr Wheeler the butcher, and Jack Smith in the village as the fishmonger and butcher, and the baker was Bromleys or the Co-op from Maidenhead, who would come round in their van.

Georgina Jones, born 1917.

Before the war

Just before the war there was a greengrocers, the International, run by 'Tacker' Aplin. Ernie Tuck used to deliver the milk in a can, and Bromley's the baker would deliver. Miss Annie Slack sold sweets and papers. She was wonderful to us children. We were allowed to sample the sweets before we bought them to see if we liked them, and any fruit that had a little bruise on she would give to us, she never sold it. The Royal Exchange pub was run by Jimmy May. He was great fun. It was a working men's pub. They had a 'slate club' – you'd pay in so much a week, and then you could take it out at Christmas, or if you were ill. You could play shove ha'penny, cards, or dominoes. They had one at the New Inn as well. Then there was a garage run by the Remingtons. I remember going to get the accumulator charged for the radio there. This was before we had electricity in the house. We would listen to the radio a lot. I listened to Children's Hour, and we had a wind-up gramophone that we used to use. We had the 'Laughing Policeman' – but I can't remember the others.

Nancy James, born 1927.

Gobstoppers

Alice Slack's shop [in the 1930s] was in the cottages where the Peking Inn is now. We used to say to each other that she was a witch

The Co-op bread van.

because she had wispy white hair underneath a very battered black velour hat that she wore all the time. She had a big black alpaca apron with a huge pocket in the front where she kept all the money. If any of us had a penny we could buy a huge gobstopper, which we would suck for a while and then take it out to see if the colour had changed! She also sold sherbet dabs, aniseed balls and liquorice rolls with an aniseed ball in the middle.

Lynda Whitworth (Pat Thompson), born 1925.

Worked together

Next door to the dairy on the High Street used to be Shergold's shop and he used to be organist at the church. It was a greengrocer and newsagents. When I first came to Cookham all the businesses and shops worked with each other. They'd all say to each other 'now, how's so and so paying up?'

and put each other wise. There used to be a garage in the yard of the Kings Arms. In the old days you couldn't leave cars parked out on the road—there were no lights. Budgens was by the Kings Arms and you could smell you were getting near to it in those days because of the smell of coffee – a lovely smell.

Eddie Smyth, born 1909.

Café society

I loved the Copper Kettle in the High Street. It was a very intimate little place; the two people who ran it were lovely. It was a very personal place where people really did meet each other. It was open all day; you could have breakfast, lunch or tea. The food was all home made. We also liked to go to the Two Roses as well. That was all home cooking too.

Ruth Charlton-Brown, born 1916.

Budgens in the High Street.

The only phone

I came to Cookham when I got married. We got married at Holy Trinity and moved straight in to Black Butts when it was new. I was the only one in Black Butts to have a phone, because my husband worked for the gas and they put it in so they could call him. I used to have everyone come round here to phone the doctor, the hospitals and whoever so I would always know what was going on. I even had somebody with her love life on the phone. We had to stop that! Once she said to me when I was going out could I leave the window open and put the phone on the windowsill so she could use it!

Connie Fenner, born 1910.

River froze over

The river froze right across while I was still living with my parents at Ferry Cottage by the bridge. We had to go and break the ice to let the traffic through. It was solid because it had built up against the bridge. Cookham Lock still had the rollers. They saved going through the lock. Punts and skiffs and dinghies could go over the rollers so the lock didn't have to be opened. In the summer they were so busy. The lock keepers were always in competition with each other to see who had the best garden.

John Brooks, born 1923.

Raced round the tarrystone

I was a baby when we moved to East Flint next to Barnside, in the High Street. My father came out of the Royal Flying Corps as a pilot and he started a taxi business. Cars were pretty scarce in those days. He also started racing GN Fraser Nash cars from our

33

The tarrystone when it was at the top of the High Street.

garage, Remingtons, in the middle of the village. I remember him practising with his hill climb cars up and down Cookham High Street. He would go up the High Street, round the tarrystone, and then down to the war memorial and back up again. The villagers weren't best pleased with him. This would be in the mid-1920s.

Peter Remington, born 1922.

The toll gate in the river

When the toll bridge was freed all the potters from Odney Pottery went up and we threw the gate that had been across the bridge in the river! We were so glad it was freed. The Wheeler family, Roy and his dad, ran that bridge for years. Before they ran the bridge Roy's mother and father ran one of the steamers on the river. They had dancing and whatever on the boats.

Leslie Knight, born 1923.

The old vicarage

When we arrived in 1954, the Westropps were living in the vicarage. The diocesan authorities said they would not maintain old properties any more and that we would have to have a new vicarage, which is why the new one was built in about 1988. There was a real struggle within the council, but eventually we decided to sell some properties that the Church owned in the village, such as the Church Hall, and two houses in the village, and we would buy the existing vicarage and paddock to use as the community centre and car park. Everyone is glad now that we did it, but there was a lot of argument at the time. The vicarage was empty for a while. It was a really cold winter, and I remember going over one day at Christmas and the pipes had all burst. The lath and plaster walling had come apart, the ceilings were down, and I was in tears. I decided, though, that it was God saying that we'd done the right thing – and that it needed to be renovated!

Rick Terry

Cookham health service

A lot of men wouldn't go to the doctors. They would just go to the chemist – Mr Henry, opposite the Kings Hall at the top of the High Street. He was very good. The men would go and say they had something wrong with their stomach or whatever, and he'd knock you a bottle of medicine up and that usually worked. The women would go to the doctor, but not the men. He was a lovely man and really good. It used to cost you 3d a week for hospital, and you were treated like lords if you went in. It cost 1s 6d a week National Deposit, and that paid for the doctors. It was an insurance scheme, and you would go to Station Road to Mr Francis to pay it. The money for the hospital you paid to Nurse Bartlett.

Ray Fenner, born 1935.

Acceptable friend

We were having breakfast one morning when it came on the wireless that sweets were coming off ration. My father produced a sixpence and challenged me to get to the Quality Shop, which was the village sweet shop, and buy a bar of chocolate so we could share it going to school. Of course I did it! Although I went to the village school I had friends among those children who went to boarding schools. I suppose because my father was headmaster I was considered acceptable! We would go on punting parties to celebrate birthdays with the more privileged children, and I do recall when I was about ten going to a big party at the hotel in Bray, with the children of the MGM staff. We wore long dresses and had bronze dancing pumps.

Enid Grant (Jenkins), born 1943.

The toll gate goes in the river, 1947.

Took cow on holiday

White Place Farm was the first place in the country to have tuberculin-tested cattle. The second Lord Astor, Waldorf, had TB and always took a cow with him when he went on holiday to make sure they had tested milk to drink. When they went to the estate in Scotland they would take half a private train to make sure they had room for the cow from White Place Farm! I was always interested in butterflies and I saw a Camberwell Beauty once outside Widbrook Cottage where I lived – now that is a rare creature. It had migrated from the continent. I remember once seeing a field of clover just south of Widbrook Common and it had more Clouded Yellow butterflies over it than whites. Again, on the Common I remember seeing a cornfield being cut and as the uncut patch got smaller there was a cluster of blue butterflies, showing how many flowers there must have been amongst the corn. That has all gone now.

John Field, born 1924.

Always get a game at the pub

We used to play darts at the Crown. In the fifties the owner would take us to Brighton once a year and Bob Monkhouse came with us once. When we first went there it had a public bar and a little bottle and jug, and then a private bar. The private bar people wouldn't mix with us lot. All the gentry would be in the private bar, and us 'yobs' would be in the public! People would come from all over to go the Cookham pubs – they were well known. We had the Ferry, Bel and the Dragon, The Royal Exchange (Maliks) , the Crown, the Kings Arms (Out and Out) , the White Hart (Spencers), The Gate (closed), and the New Inn (Swan Uppers). That was a real spit and sawdust pub, but spotlessly clean. In the fifties that was run by Rene Astor, and her Mum and Dad. You could go in at any time and get a game of something, darts, dominoes, crib, solo, shove ha'penny. The Kings Arms used to have a big hall outside and they had bar billiards and all sorts. They all had a public and a private bar.

White Place Farm boasts of 'clean milk' in the 1930s.

Floods can be fun! Cookham in 1947.

The working men would drink mild beer, dark beer, but the gentry always had half a bitter! The working men's club opened over a hundred years ago, and is still there as the social club by the station.

Ray Fenner, born 1935.

The floods

I was here for the floods in 1954 when I was working during the week at Moor Hall. We would have to take a punt to get up the High Street. I remember helping Mrs Baker at the Kings Arms to get out the barrels from the cellar where they were just floating around. John Grover went to the bar there one day, and started chatting to the barman, Tony Welling, and discovered that he was an ordained priest who had not been able to get a parish. He hauled him out of the bar and took him on at Holy Trinity.

Rick Terry

Wellies in the loo

I remember when the floods were very bad in 1947 we had to go to school in a boat. It even trickled over the causeway. Gran's toilet was outside and the water was lapping up the steps. You had to wear your wellies to go to the toilet!

Jeanette Roll (Edwards) born 1941.

Furniture lost

During the 1947 floods we were woken up by the police at five o'clock in the morning and told we had an hour to move our furniture. They came up very suddenly. When we went to bed that night the water was out on the common, but not very much. We had had a very hard winter and it had thawed very quickly. We couldn't get much stuff upstairs because our stairs have a bend in them, and you can't get anything up them. Mr Fairchild and Mr Davis, who were the builders across

The Moor floods, January 1925.

the way, brought us some bricks and planks. We lost our three-piece suite and lots of furniture. Furniture was on dockets [coupons] in those days and we lost such a lot. It was in for three weeks, and it was two feet deep. We had an open fire upstairs that has two little hobs on it, where my mother did all the cooking. They used to get the food brought by boat. The baker would deliver by boat.

Nancy James, born 1927.

in Maidenhead. One of father's businesses in the winter was pulling cars and lorries out of the floods. We had a special vehicle to do it and when that didn't work we would have to get the shire horses out to do it. We'd tow it back to the garage and the magneto was always full of water. My father would take them off, clean them out and dry them in the oven in the kitchen. It was an oil-fired oven, and we had no electric light in those days.

Peter Remington, born 1922.

Father helped out

It was very much colder in the winter, and I seem to remember always getting flooded. We would go for walks in the flooded areas and mother used to buy me a new pair of boots every flood because I would get them so wet. When the floods froze we could skate all over the place. I have skated all the way to Bourne End one way and up Strande Water the other. You could get down to Bridge Road

Flower festival

I became church warden at Holy Trinity in 1976, and did the job for twelve years. There was a flower festival in 1975 and I was on the Committee. We had twenty or thirty ladies arranging flowers. Lois Ashwandon actually had some flowers flown in from the then Rhodesia [Zimbabwe] for the festival. She had relatives living out there, and she phoned BOAC and got them to bring over some 'Bird of Paradise' flowers. No one had ever seen anything like it before, and many were convinced they were plastic.

Rick Terry

The Kings Hall

When I was younger you never thought to go up to Cookham Dean, unless it was for something specific. You'd never think to go there. We sometimes go up the Chequers. The boys in Cookham Dean used to belong to the Scouts. We'd use the Kings Hall [Stanley Spencer Gallery] for Scouts and all sorts of different things, like weddings and parties. It was the village hall and a real meeting place for people.

Ray Fenner, born 1935.

The Kings Hall – which houses the Stanley Spencer Gallery – as it is today

For the people

The Kings Hall was given to the people of the Village as a reading room – it shouldn't have been used for the gallery. We used to have whist drives, there, and the guides would use it. We'd go up the Church Hall sometimes (by Westwood Green), but the Kings Hall was for our end of the village.

Connie Fenner, born 1910.

Memorial seat

Michael Briggs and I were friends. He was always keen on aeroplanes. He lived in the Cookham Road in Walnut Tree Cottage. He had a summerhouse in the garden and built a beautiful model of an airliner in balsa wood, and he was going to tow it behind his bicycle. It had a petrol engine. I helped him build this for a long time, and then I was shipped off to

Eastbourne to live for a while and we lost touch. He died in the war, and the tarrystone used to have a plaque on the side. His mother had the seat put there as a memorial.

Peter Remington, born 1922.

The Cookham Society

The Cookham Society formed for two reasons in 1969. The Astor family had moved away from Cliveden and put White Place Farm up for sale and, being totally over gravel deposits, it was bought by a gravel company. They proposed to put in a massive development. At the same time a planning application came in for developing Poundfield and the Cookham Society was formed to oppose them. We raised a lot of money and employed a QC and beat Ready Mix Concrete, who had never lost an application before. About ten years later there was an

Jean Stretton and fellow members of the Cookham Society.

application for a leisure complex, but that would have meant gravel extraction as well. It's still owned by the gravel company, but at least we made them stop and think. The character of the Village would have changed totally if either development had gone ahead. The Society now works to improve the Village. It does not oppose change for the sake of it.

John Field, born 1924.

Bel and the Dragon

Bel and the Dragon was run by people called Wilkinson when I remember it first. Then it was taken over in the late thirties by a man who had been head-waiter at the Savoy, and his clientele came with him. At weekends there would be stage people, and he would write on a piece of paper who was in, and I would come and join my father and have a good look. I remember seeing John Mills one time and Rex Harrison and his wife Lily Palmer.

Sonia Redway, born 1927.

The local

I'd go to the Royal Exchange with the church choir, but when that changed a bit we tended to move to the Crown, where there was dear old Bert Wootten, who lived in a cottage in the High Street. Bert used to say 'You can't be a local if you haven't got grandparents in the churchyard'. I remember he came round to the church once with me and he had what he called a 'two man' screwdriver, which was about five feet long. He'd made it to tighten the new screws, which he'd put in the south door to the church.

Rick Terry.

Minding the commons

When I was growing up we had a Hayward on the commons by the name of George Allen. He always wore a bowler hat and he used to have a pony and trap. His job was to look after the commons and especially the cattle when they were in the season. He knew whose cows were whose, although they were all just branded with a big stamp: W for Widbrook and C for Cockmarsh. He had a walking stick with a wide chisel on the end of it, which he used to cut down thistles. Widbrook opened on the 14 May – Widbrook Fair day. George Allen would have his little tar pot on a fire and there was always a policeman and the clerk to the parish council to collect the money

James Hatch, born 1930.

The National Trust

The National Trust took over the commons in 1934, and there was a management committee. I joined that committee in 1963. It used to have rather more powers than it does now. We had to decide whether to go on cultivating the commons. Before the war none of the commons had been cultivated, and during the war large areas of Cookham Dean Common, Pinkney's Green and The Thicket were ploughed up to grow crops. There was much discussion after the war and it was decided, I think regrettably, that as grazing couldn't be carried out on the land that had been cleared because of it's proximity to roads, hay should be grown, and the commoners who had rights of grazing should have the hay instead.

John Field, born 1924.

Winter Hill is maintained by the National Trust.

Friendly place

My first impression of Cookham was that it was lovely and a very friendly place. You have to join things in order to get to know people. My mother's impression of it was that it was very unfriendly, because people didn't drop by and come in. With the war we were all so busy running various organizations that people didn't have time for such things. My sister ran a riding-stables at the back of Rowborough and we would have house parties to cut the hay from the fields.

Vivien Jerome (Mrs Ripley), born 1909.

Nobody talks

I've lived here all these years, and everybody used to be friendly. Now nobody knows anybody, and nobody speaks to anybody. Now nobody speaks to you. I know a couple of people who live in Black Butts, but that's it.

Connie Fenner, born 1910.

Atmosphere has changed

Being brought up in Widbrook Cottages on the Common, I lived in a place where you saw so many wild creatures. The majority of the water birds that relied on boggy ground have moved as the land has dried up. Snipe and Redshank used to nest on Cockmarsh, and to a certain extent the Lapwing. There was a wonderful man called Edmund Giles who lived in Cookham Dean who would tell me where to go and look for certain birds. Cockmarsh has always been my favourite area, but it has changed beyond all recognition. It may not have changed physically much, but the atmosphere is different these days.

John Field, born 1924.

4 Life in Cookham Rise

Life at the Gate

My grandfather was landlord at the Gate in the Pound. As a little girl I was always allowed in the public bar. I remember the old boys that were there – Tommy Jones, Billy Chalfont, and Ned who was as deaf as a post but was a wizard at playing dominoes. I learnt to play crib and dominoes. It was always called the Gate Hotel although it was really just a country pub. The swinging sign outside on the corner had a picture of a five barred gate and green fields, and said:

This gate hangs high and hinders none
Refresh and pay and travel on.

It had a saloon bar and a public bar. The saloon bar was considered very up market, with Lloyd Loom chairs and round tables with glass tops. The two bars were separated by a wooden partition with a stained glass screen. The drinks cost less in the public bar. The market gardeners from Westwood Green and the field where the nursery school is now would come in to the Gate after work, wearing trousers tied round the knee with string and caps on their heads. Grandfather had a huge

The Gate Hotel.

reputation for having really good beer. He used to have to carry barrels of beer up thirteen stone steps from the cellar. The beer had to settle and be tapped and attended to, which was very critical for the keeping of it.

Lynda Whitworth (Pat Thompson), born 1925.

The Railway Tavern

My mother and father, Mary and Eric Rance, came to Cookham in 1968 to run the Railway Tavern by the station. It was a real local pub, and the darts, dominoes and cribbage teams were really competitive. People would come down from the Dean and up from the village and meet in The Railway in the Rise. The sign outside had a picture of the steam train, the 'Cookham Manor', that

used to run on the Marlow branch line. It was the brewery that suggested they change the name to The Cookham Tavern. When my father retired in 1981 it signalled an end to the real old characters that ran the pubs in that era. There was Colonel at the Chequers, Barbara and Harold at the Royal Exchange and Cynthia at the New Inn. It's all very different now.

Marilyn Rothwell.

Grandparents ran the off-licence

Father was born in to a family of five children who lived in Ross Cottage, Graham Road. They used to call it Gramophone Road, because it was one of the first roads where

Mary and Eric Rance in the mid-1970s

Lower Road, Cookham Rise.

nearly everybody had a gramophone. In the late twenties our grandparents ran the off-licence at the corner of New Road in Cookham Rise. It operated as a general store and our mother helped in the shop as a young girl, weighing out sugar currants and raisins in pounds and ounces and wrapping them up in brown paper. She measured out the beer, which they sold by the jug-full.

Keith and Barry Hatch, born 1932 and 1935.

Take your own towel

Mrs Gallagher ran the hairdressers next to the chemists in Cookham Rise. Just after the war you could always tell when someone was going to see Mrs Gallagher, because they would walk up the road with a towel over their arm. She didn't supply towels, she hadn't got the soap to wash them – so you took your own. Next door to her was Mrs Robinson, the chemist, and across the road was Greens the shoe shop. Next to them were Miss Woodbridge and Miss Brazil, who ran a wool shop. That was before Mrs Lake took it over. Mrs Lake was a widow with three children who lived over the shop. She had everything, and could always find it, and was always giving you advice about what you needed!

Margaret Tuck, born 1937.

You could always get what you wanted

Mr King's was a treasure-trove. If you wanted anything, you would go to Mr King and he would get it. I think he had been a very upright man, but with age he had stooped. In the war you couldn't get hairnets or things like that-but he would always manage to get them for you.

Joan Stringer, born 1922.

Thursday closing

Mr King would always go up to London on Thursdays to get his parcels. He sold absolutely everything. He had a cellar, and was often popping down there to get things. Mrs King used to run the shop on a Thursday morning, and like everywhere else it was early closing on a Thursday. They had a daughter and they called her 'Queenie'. The next shop along was Shackles Laundry, and then there was Pinder Hall.

Margaret Tuck, born 1937.

Oxford and Cambridge

We'd buy our presents from Mr King's shop – we called him 'William Whitely' after the store in London. I believe he was the first one to have a television before the war. We always went there to get our Oxford and Cambridge favours. Everyone in the village would be for one side or the other.

John Taft, born 1921.

Wonderful butcher

Mrs Swatton was a dear lady who ran the corner shop. She was called Vera and he was Viv. It was only a tiny shop, but she kept everything, including frozen cat food. She loved cats. Her fresh vegetables were handpicked. If I came home from work late she would stay open for me, or I could phone and ask her to put out things for me and she would. I used Mr Wheeler as my butcher – he killed his own. He never cleared up after himself; if you asked for steak, he'd leave the piece out. He'd quarrel with his wife all the time, but his meat was wonderful. My son would deliver meat for him on a Saturday, and he'd pay him with a bit of steak. The

Bill and Winifred Wheeler in 1974.

butcher had an assistant called Roy, and he gave my son a tip. They had to deliver meat to Lord Meston up Bradcutts Lane, and he had a big dog. Roy told my son to take a bone with him and then throw it as far as he could to keep the dog occupied while he delivered the meat!

Dorothy Campe, born 1913.

Blocks of ice for the meat

Arthur Palmer, the butcher up in Cookham Rise, didn't have a fridge. He had an icebox, and the iceman used to come with great big blocks of ice. He had massive tongs and he would manhandle the blocks of ice into the box. He used to chain smoke, always had a cigarette in the corner of his mouth.

Ray Fenner, born 1935.

High-class grocers

Next door to Pinder Hall was Mr Gallagher's, the gentleman's hairdressers. His wife was on one side of the road, and he was on the other. He did shaves as well. Then it was Mrs Wilson's, a 'high class' grocers. We knew it was because there was a sign on the wall where we used to play ball, which told us so. Next along was the post office, run by Mrs Sullivan. They had a little sorting office, where they would sort the post in the morning. Down towards the station was the little hut, which is now a shoe-repair shop. That was run by Mrs Sale and her husband, and they would sell sweets and newspapers. Websters was next door and then opposite, in what is now Station Parade, was the Gribbin's grocery shop. They used to cook their own beetroots. You could always smell when they were doing that. They had a little nursery in Graham Road, where they would grow things to sell.

Margaret Tuck, born 1937.

Westwood Green

When we first lived on Westwood Green the baker came three times a week; the butcher came, the greengrocer came twice a week, and a grocer came once a week. They came round with paraffin, with wet fish and dry cleaning. Mr Sims, the greengrocer on the High Street, had a Mynah bird. This bird had learnt how to mimic air brakes on a lorry, and it would make this horrendous noise. People would fall over the potatoes when he let out this shriek. There wasn't much room in the shop, it was very small and very crowded. The International was a great shop too. On a Wednesday afternoon you could put your list in for your shopping, and on a Friday afternoon the old chap would come round and give you your box of shopping for a shilling. This would be in the sixties.

Margaret Terry.

Seaton Cottage

My granddad Ash came up from Devon in about 1900 and he married Laura Jane Tuck, who was a sister of William, who ran the dairy in the village. They had four children, two boys and two girls. Uncle Ernie ran the dairy in Cookham Rise. I married one of the Cookham Dean Tucks, Harry. When I remember Uncle Ernie Tuck, he had the dairy at Elm Villa in Cookham Rise. He would take me to White Place Farm to get the milk. The dairy was really just a big garage at the side of the house, with two big sinks. He would bottle up the milk there. They stopped getting it from White Place eventually because of pasteurisation. He did like a drink, and when he eventually got a car it was always scratched.

Margaret Tuck (Ash), born 1937.

Building the Methodist Hall

To raise money to build the Wesley Hall behind the Methodist Chapel in 1928 there was a scheme they called the mile of pennies. At that time the Sunday school was held in a tin hut on the side which was getting dilapidated. People volunteered to give a penny or so a week towards fundraising, which I used to go round and collect on Saturday mornings when I was about twelve. I collected £25 and had my name put on the board.

Lucy Edwards, born 1914.

Laura Jane Ash (on the right) enjoys a day out with friends.

First death

My grandmother was run over and killed by a motorbike in 1937 outside the Methodist Hall. I think she was the first person killed in a motor accident in Cookham. Her name was Laura Jane Ash. They lived at Hillside Cottages. Grandma was killed on a Saturday afternoon as she crossed the road. Nobody really explained how it happened.

Margaret Tuck, born 1937.

Buttonholes for the commuters

In the window of Websters Corn Chandlers in Station Hill they had a border done in a diamond pattern, made out of all different kinds of grain. They sold corn, maize, logs and potatoes. Westwood Green at the time [1930s] was all market gardening for Websters. Opposite was a little corrugated iron shed that sold flowers. She sold buttonholes for the men going up to London in the steam trains.

Lynda Whitworth, born 1925.

When Cookham was an important station

When my husband ran the railway station, you could have eaten off the floor of the signal box. The waiting room always had a roaring fire when it was cold, and the gardens were immaculate. There were three different signalmen, in shifts, and they all had pride. All the levers were shone up and it used to be so spic and span. He was stationmaster in the mid-fifties, and did the job until Dr Beeching's axe fell in the mid-sixties. After the Cookham stationmaster's job went he worked all over the place. When there were

Steaming into Cookham station.

two lines running through Cookham it was an important station. He used to have to be down at the station for the first business train at 7.30 a.m. He would have a break at lunchtime, and then go back. Often he would go down at night to lock up, and he often did weekends as well. There was very bad snow once, and he had to go down and dig out the level crossing. The trains were very regular, always ran on time, and you could get one every quarter of an hour. He had a uniform, a navy blue suit, and he hated his hat – so you never saw him in a uniform because he wouldn't wear it!

Joan Stringer, born 1922.

The footbridge

The station was lovely. There was nice waiting room with a cosy stove in it, which kept going all day. I remember Mr Stringer,

the stationmaster. The signalman lived at the end of the station. The driver would have to hand over a key to the signalman to control the line for the next train to come through. There was a footbridge over the track, joining the two platforms. There were gates on the level crossing and I remember there was a big protest when they were removed.

Stanley Jones, born 1914.

Accident at level crossing

I was on the Marlow train when it had an accident. At the level crossing people had to get out and open a big gate, then go back and get your car, then close the gate, and there was another one to open. If you got caught on the railway line, then you would get hit. Well, I was on the train once, just outside the bridge over the railway, and it hit a car. Two people were killed. I felt the bump, and the train just took the car along the track.

Dorothy Campe, born 1913.

New pathway

When we arrived in Romanlea the road was not built up, it was just a mass of puddles. So one Sunday morning the men all got together and got a cement mixer and started to make a path. It was a most awful day and the rain was bucketing down. It was a right to-do – all these women making all these cups of tea for all these men! We shopped a lot at Mrs Durham's. There was Norman's, the paper shop next door. Station Parade was built in the 1960s. By that time, Westwood Green and Southwood Gardens had been built, so we needed more shops. When we first moved in 1951, Cookham was very small and you really knew everybody, at least to say hello to in the street.

Georgina Jones, born 1917.

PC Tubb.

The building starts

Opposite Pinder Hall was a lovely field with a barn in it. That's where Coxborrow Close was built. When the building started, Westwood Green was first. People hated it. We didn't know about planning in those days, and it just suddenly appeared. The land was all owned by Mr Martin, who built Westwood Green. He owned Station Parade too, and it had lots of advertising hoardings all round it.

Margaret Tuck (Ash), born 1937.

Life as the copper's son

There wasn't a lot of major crime in the village. It was strange though that my father, who was the local copper, couldn't go in the local pubs. We could never have people in the house and I don't ever remember having a friend come in to see me at the police house. It just wasn't done for the village policeman to have any connection with the villagers. The only connection they could have was going to church. We had to be virtually isolated from the people in the village. Sergeant Tocock would cycle ten miles, to go and have a drink in a pub outside the village.

John Tubb, born 1928.

Knew who done it

If anybody did anything wrong, their mum and dad would ask Constable Tubb to have a word with them and he would. If anything did go on in the village he usually knew who had done it. They knew everybody in the village, the poachers, burglars or scrumpers!

Doreen Tubb (Harris), born 1926.

Political party

In 1951 there were about 150 members of the Labour Party. We used to collect their subs, about 6d a week, I think. The children were very small and Stanley, my husband, went along to Pinder Hall where they were having a party and there were dozens of children running around and making a noise, and it was very different from what we were used to. It was at the time when the post-war Labour government was trying to get the National Health Service up and running, and we were keen to support it.

Georgina Jones, born 1917.

Controversy at the parish council

When I was on the parish council, the biggest thing we had to deal with was the Alfred Major playing fields. It was given to the parish in 1947 to be developed as a recreation ground, and plans were drawn up about what was going to be on it – and then nothing happened. It just stayed as a field for years and years. Then a few people put a few bits of apparatus there for children to play on, and the football club played there – but the rest of it was left as it was. It was only cut about two or three times a year. Then some of these people, like me, thought there should be something on there. That was what it was given for. We had public meetings at the school about it and it all got very heated.

Stanley Jones, born 1914.

5 Life in Cookham Dean

Local shopping

My mother used to shop locally as much as possible. Kathy Ricketts had the Enterprise Store opposite the Chequers, and you could get vegetables from there. What with the Miss Pryors' post office stores, George Pearce the butcher, and bread which was delivered by Ken Deadman, whose father owned Carmonta, you didn't have to go too far. Paraffin and methylated for the primus would be delivered by Mr Church in Cookham.

Gordon Harris, born 1932.

Meeting place

'Daddy' Wilson ran a shop on the end of Royal Cottages on the Village Green. He was the local barber and also sold newspapers and comics. I got 6d for doing the paper round for him. He was open every night until ten o'clock, and my grandfather would go over twice a week to get his shave. It was a real meeting place for local people.

Pat Woodbridge, born 1927.

The Carmonta Bakery shop in the 1950s.

The dairy shop at the side of the Jolly Farmer c. 1925.

Milk from the pub

Mr Palmer, the butcher, would come up to Cookham Dean from Cookham Rise (now The Old Butcher's Shop) with the meat delivery on his horse and cart. Mother and I would have walked down to his shop on Lower Road to place the order and pay, I remember the sawdust on the floor. The baker was Mr Deadman and he would deliver either with his van or horse and cart. We got our milk from Mr and Mrs Hollyer at the Jolly Farmer. The milk came from churns – you would hand over your jug and they'd fill it with a ladle. They had a little shop at the side of the pub which was for dairy produce

Frances Harvey, born 1918.

Ice creams too

When I went to get the milk from the Jolly Farmer the girls used to laugh at me because there was a lamb in the garden that used to frighten me! They sold ice creams, and they used to have pigs and a couple of cows there as well.

Nancy Harvey, born 1916.

Nothing private

When Miss Gertie Deadman kept the post office at Cookham Dean, she sold lots of things there. If there were telegrams going out and coming in she would leave the counter and walk to the telephone which was in the middle of the shop so that everybody could hear!

Frances Harvey, born 1918.

Late-night opening

Pryors Shop down in Cookham Dean Bottom used to stay open until ten o'clock at night, run by the two Miss Pryors. It was a post office and general store, and my grandfather

Gigg's butchers shop in Dean Lane in the 1950s.

Harry used to go down there to buy his insurance stamps. He'd go down about eight o'clock. The letterbox is still in the wall. The only Cookham Dean butcher was George Pearce at the bottom of Warners Hill.

Pat Woodbridge, born 1927.

The pig killer

Everybody had pigs... Colonel down the Chequers had one, they had them up at Easts, by the coal yard behind the shop. That was something I enjoyed doing, going round with the pig killer. Harry would kill his pig and hang it in the trees. The pig killer came from Maidenhead and his name was Tom Hicks.

Ray Nash, born 1929.

The pubs

Lots of people would go to the pub. They were real meeting places, particularly for the gardeners. The Jolly Farmer was the main village pub, even though the 'Hare and Hounds' [Inn on the Green] was bigger. They had a saloon bar and a public bar. I think it was a law that you had to have that. The public bar was very basic with plain wood tables and chairs, but the prices were cheaper. Dennis Hearman was landlord at the 'Hare and Hounds' and started food there for the first time. He'd cook steak sandwiches and things in the late fifties, and people would come up from a long way off Fridays and Saturdays to watch the cricket on the Green and have one of his famous sandwiches.

Ray Lewington, born 1939.

Regulars

My father, Dud, would go for a drink regularly every Saturday night, Sunday lunchtime and Sunday evening. What he would do would be to go to the 'Hare and Hounds' first, have a pint there and then he'd come to the Jolly

Farmer on the way home, so he'd get there about half past eight on the Saturday night. He would go with Fred Dyer, Den Taft, Fred Woodbridge and Jim Ricketts.

Jack Tomlin, born 1927.

Sign to start

Jack's dad would come in on the Saturday night and have bread and cheese and pickles. That was the signal for everybody else to have them too. Nobody would have it until he'd had his. If he was late everybody would be looking round for him – because nobody would eat before him! We had a famous regular once, Ronnie Howard used to live in Old Ducketts, and his dad was Leslie Howard. Ron used to be in films too, and looked just like his dad. He played cricket for Cookham Dean once or twice.

John Tubb, born 1928.

Hare and Hounds

As a boy I used to go to the 'jug and bottle' entrance at the 'Hare and Hounds' and collect my grandmother's jug of stout. There was a hatch round the side of the pub which is on the foot path, so you didn't have to go in to the actual pub. There were very many characters around. 'Long Harry' Parsons was a local carpenter and builder, and Sid Startin was a real rogue – bit of a beggar. He lived in School Road. Of course there was Ted Wakeling. My grandfather Harry was very well known. He was a lovely man – never heard him raise his voice and he would always help people out.

Pat Woodbridge, born 1927.

The Chequers

The Copas's used to run the Chequers, but the Garretts ran it when we arrived in 1939. Mum and dad, plus Percy and his sister. Why they called him 'Colonel' I don't know… everybody loved that pub. It was a proper village pub and you could play darts and dominoes and cribbage and all the villagers went in there. It used to be packed out.

Mabel Vevers.

John Taft with the cows in the orchard at the back of the Jolly Farmer in 1927.

The old village hall comes down.

Uncle Tom's

My dad used to tell a story about the men of
Cookham Dean when he was a lad of about
sixteen. All the poachers and baddies up the
Dean used to meet at Uncle Tom's. Now
there was only one policeman who had to do
Cookham and Cookham Dean and they had
a habit of meeting him as he would come up
the hill and taking him in to the pub for a
drink. He would have so many that he would
be completely sloshed and couldn't move.
Then they'd all go out poaching – and the
next day go round the village selling their
rabbits and pheasants.

Leslie Knight, born 1923.

The Kaffirs return

I remember being in the Jolly Farmer when
the Kaffirs fundraising group was re-started. It
was before 1976, but I can't quite remember
when. A football match was arranged if I
remember right. A proper Kaffir is someone

born and bred in Cookham Dean. They say
they were named after the cherries but I
think it was after the Boer War. There was a
saying 'you're a right little kaffir', and that
meant you were a right little demon and it
stuck. They used to have concerts in the
Young Men's Club in Cookham Dean. The
original Kaffirs would organize them. Jack
Tomlin's Aunt Hilda used to sing 'Mother
Macree' and Gladys Clegg used to sing
'Cherry Ripe' up in the Drill Hall. That's
where the Kaffirs would have their concert
parties. They pulled it down to build the new
village hall.

Doreen Tubb, born 1926.

Cricket and football

We would play cricket and football on the
village green, the Cricket Common. The
football club started in 1879 in Cookham
Dean, but in those early days they didn't play
competitive football, just local friendlies.
Most people worked till one o'clock on

Saturday, so Saturday afternoon was the only time they could play football. When the cricket team started they played down the Hockett. It's rumoured that the cricket club started in the 1860s – but we've found no proof of it. I remember there was always a crowd when I watched cricket on the common. They had a scoreboard on a stand. There was no pavilion so you just sat on the grass, and the outfield was never cut – so the grass got really long. About forty or fifty would turn out to watch the cricket – but for the football sometimes you'd get crowds of about two or three hundred. Volunteers would look after the wicket. Albert Gough who lived in Popes Lane was one I remember well, but everybody helped. We would all just muck in. Mr Simmonds was the vicar when I was a lad in Cookham Dean, and he was a great football and cricket supporter. He would never conduct a wedding on a Saturday because he always wanted to come and watch the match. We used to call Mr

Simmonds 'Old Soapy' – I don't know why.

Pat Woodbridge, born 1927.

Local competition

It used to be a bit of a competition between the local 'gentry' who could put on the best show. They used to organize cricket teams to play the local lads, and always put on a lunch or a tea in a marquee or in their gardens. Sides would come from all over to play us because it was such a wonderful place to play. When I first remember the Cricket Common there was a barn on the corner of the road going up to the Hare and Hounds, and the groundsman, Albert Gough used to keep his equipment there. In the mid-1950s we needed to build a pavilion so we got a grant, and local people were very generous and we built our pavilion. There were lots of people watching the cricket. Eventually as the houses got built the cricket balls became a problem. Mr Gummer,

Dr Stone and the team in 1910.

who lived on the common, always did his gardening with a tin helmet on because he didn't want to stop the cricket.

Ray Lewington, born 1939.

New pavilion

I spent hours and hours building the new pavilion. We spent every Sunday morning for weeks and weeks in Jim Ricketts barn at Hardings Green building it. I did it with Fred Dyer. 'Colonel' Percy Garrett did the brick work and we got a firm to put the shingles on. It was quite difficult playing cricket on the common. The ball would often go through windows, and it was my job to mend the glass. The worst trouble I got in was at Thornbury Cottage. Someone put a ball through the window when they were sitting watching the television.

John Taft, born 1921.

The other pavilion

I lived and worked at Moor Hall during the war. One of the dormitories down there at the time is now the Cookham Dean Cricket Club pavilion at Ricketts Wicket. They were wooden dormitories and they just moved parts of them up to the Club.

Pat Woodbridge, born 1927.

Cottages gentrified

I was inducted on 21 April 1971. When I arrived there were two sorts of people: old people, mostly widows, living in big houses and there were many people who had been born and worked in the area. They lived in little cottages of which there aren't many left; most have been gentrified. I remember one man who had worked as a gardener, but as a boy he had worked cleaning knives in the

The opening ceremony for the cricket pavilion on the Common in 1957.

vicarage. We lived in the old vicarage when we first came but it was very cold.

Revd John Copping, born 1934.

Built the church

My grandmother and grandfather went to the Methodist Chapel down by the Chalk Pit, which at the time was the only church in Cookham Dean. My grandfather had originally been Catholic. One day in 1840 a parson came round and said he wanted to build a church in Cookham Dean, and as my grandfather was a stonemason he employed him to do it.

Leslie Knight, born 1923

Dissenters

The Methodist chapel was still open when I first came here. It had been built slightly before the church and there is a letter in the archives from the vicar of Cookham (Cookham Dean was in the parish of Cookham then) to the Bishop of Oxford talking about the 'late intrusions of the dissenters' i.e. the Methodists were here and so they were in a hurry to get the church up and running! The subscription list of our church is headed by the Dowager Queen Adelaide and all the local gentry and then you get a few villagers, not many. This is in contrast with the Methodists who were a group of working men who got a loan and raised the money themselves.

Revd John Copping, born 1934.

Sang in the choir

I used to have to sing in the choir on Sunday. Mother made you go. The choir outings were quite an event. We went to Bognor, Selsey and Little Hampton. We would leave at half past six in Mr Chaster's coach. He lived down by the Chequers. His daughter was in the choir. Breakfast would be at Romsey, and then we'd spend the day on the beach. The choir was involved in the Choral Society that was run by Mrs Rowe from Dean Croft, and each year we would do a nativity play for school. We'd go carol singing too at Christmas. I'd go with my two friends, Alan Tomlin and Bill Glenister. Alan Tomlin's mother would count out the pennies so we all got the same.

John Taft, born 1921.

The big event

As little children at Christmas we would hang up my dad's sock and be thrilled when we got an apple, an orange, a sugar mouse and a pencil. My father had a brother who worked on a big estate in Derbyshire and every year he would send us a rabbit for Christmas. It would come through the post and we really looked forward to it for our Christmas lunch. The big event of the year for the Sunday school was a trip out to Burnham Beeches – that was lovely. There was a penny stall, amongst all the other stalls, where you could buy all sorts of things. We would go by open charabanc, walk around the Beeches and then have tea at Wingroves.

Frances Harvey, born 1918.

The buses

The buses used to run from about seven to seven-thirty in the morning till eleven o'clock at night and I remember it being 6d single, 9d return... Now we only get one or two a week. There was always a driver and a conductor on them too...

Mabel Vevers.

The choir with the Revd Simmonds in 1933.

Three bus routes

The Chequers pub was the terminus for one of the bus routes. There were three bus routes from Cookham to Maidenhead and I used to go to the Chequers to get the bus for school. The Premier bus ran along by the river – Mr Chastle at Cookham Dean had three little red buses that stopped at the Chequers and ran three times an hour to Maidenhead. There were open top buses from Cookham Dean Church to Pinkneys Green and Furze Platt.

Frances Harvey, born 1918.

The old chapel

There used to be a building at the top of Popes Lane which we called the old chapel. They pulled it down in 1955. In the photograph opposite, my father, Walter William, is up on the roof, Ted Skegg who was Mr Frost's chauffeur is on the ladder, and the one in the front is Albert Gough. He was caretaker at the Young Men's Club (Village Hall) and

lived in Popes Lane. My father went to Cookham Dean school, and left when he was twelve. Most of his education was done at night. He went to the old chapel at the top of Popes Lane. The boys used to go there in the evenings for lessons, and he learnt to read and write better than I could. In my time the old chapel was used by Frosts for an apple store. Frost owned twenty-eight houses in the area and much of the land. They only farmed fruit, Bramley apples and cherries mainly. He died in the 1960s and everything was sold off. It was sometimes known as the Studio.

John Taft, born 1921.

The doctor

I was at school at Cookham Dean, but I had been very ill and the doctor said I was too weak to walk there. Dr Shepard used to wear a top hat and tails. If he didn't wear his top hat he had a grey Homburg and he had very thick glasses. He was a gentleman – you could tell by his manner. I can still see him – he had beautiful grey wavy hair, and he had a lovely calm quiet manner. He was a lovely man.

Lucy Edwards, born 1914.

The doctor's wife

Zoe Shepard lived opposite the church in Lynwood. Her husband was the local doctor and his surgery was in fact attached to the house. She lived in very reduced circumstances although she always wanted the best of everything. She was artistic, musical and had lived a very interesting life. I believe that house had the first central heating installed in the village. We've got Dr Shepard's account books and I think what he did, he charged people who could afford it more than those who couldn't.

Revd John Copping, born 1934.

The patient

I was about six when I climbed over the railings into school going after a tennis ball, playing cricket out in the front. It was a spiked metal fence, and I slipped and got caught. Jack East lived in one of the old cottages across the road came and hoisted me off and took me down to old Dr Shepard. He was as blind as a bat, but was quite nice though. He couldn't see a thing!

John Taft, born 1921.

Trouble with the boys

When they had a fête in Marlow the boys from Cookham Dean would go and cause trouble – and the same thing happened when there was a fête in Cookham Dean. The Marlow boys would come looking for revenge. The same thing used to happen between the boys of the Dean and the Village. My father used to run down to the railway station to the paper shop to get the paper for his dad and he had to run really quickly through Cookham Rise or the boys would go after him. You would only go down

Taking down the old chapel in Popes Lane, 1955.

to the village in pairs.

Leslie Knight, born 1923.

Villages divided

Cookham Dean and Cookham were more or less divided. Our father used to tell stories about how every Saturday night gangs of hooligans used to go out just with the intention of having a good punch up. There was quite a lot of animosity between Cookham and Cookham Dean.

Keith and Barry Hatch, born 1932 and 1935.

Differences

The Cookham boys never had anything to do with the boys of Cookham Dean. The Cookham lads all went down to Odney swimming, while the Dean boys would play cricket or football in the Dean.

John Tubb, born 1928.

Bonfire night

We would swim down by Wootten's boat yard sometimes, but it's true we didn't swim much. We would go to the swimming pool towards Marlow, where the Scout camp is now. There was a roped off area and a couple of changing rooms. I used to play cricket on Bigfrith Common. It was like a separate community down there, with lots of boys. We'd have a really big bonfire on Bonfire Night. We used to start building it in September, by cutting gorse off the common. Before it was dug over in the war it was all covered in hawthorn and gorse and bracken. It was a haven for birds, and people would come out from London just to listen to them. There were greenfinches, goldfinches, long-tail-tits, everything.

Jack Tomlin, born 1927.

The nightingales

My mum used to take a blanket and we would go up to the big common just at dusk, and we'd listen to the nightingales and smell the honeysuckle. It was beautiful. I used to love cherry time too when I was little, watching them put those huge great ladders up against the trees. We would run round eating all the cherries because there were thousands and thousands of them. It was lovely. I never went cherry picking – that was men's work

Doreen Tubb, born 1926.

Skew Corner

I was born in Hockett Corner in 1929. The whole of Hockett lane was one big ditch and we could play on the corner as there were no cars, only the butcher and baker who would deliver in their vans. When we weren't in the lane we were always out playing on the common. The bracken and brambles at Skew Corner and Hartwells were ideal nesting for nightingales then. It was beautiful to hear them singing on summer nights. This was destroyed in the 1950s when the area was forested.

Ray Nash, born 1929

How it should be

It was how a village should be. If anyone was ill there was always someone to help, they would get lighting wood or shopping errands. In my opinion that is how a village should be and always ought to be.

Gordon Harris, born 1932.

6 Earning a Living

The High Street baker

My father Mr Francis was a baker in Cookham High Street and it wasn't an easy life. They were always hard at it. I remember my mother saying that my father was either in the bakehouse, sleeping, or in the Wesleyan chapel. We only had one water tap for the bakehouse and the household. Our kitchen was way beyond the bakehouse, so it was a most inconvenient living. We had the big shop and a very large living room behind, and then came the bakehouse and the kitchen, and then there were the stables for the horses and a big flour mill. My older brother always remembers him dressing a millstone, but I think the mill became redundant during the war.

Kate Swan, born 1911.

Mr Francis, the High Street baker.

The Francis Bakery bill had a very ornate heading.

Delivering the bread

In the school holidays we'd help to deliver the bread. We had bicycles and bread baskets and sometimes we'd go over My Lady Ferry on the boat to deliver to the cottages. The water could be very rough. Going to school at Holy Trinity we used to have to deliver hot rolls to Lady Redwood, who lived at the top of the street, for her breakfast. We disliked doing it! On the way home we would stop at the dairy to get the milk for baking and that was in a big tin can with a wire handle, and I always remember how that used to cut your fingers. My father started off with horses and carts but when he decided to go in for automatic things he bought a fleet of five Brooke Bonds little red Trojan cars. They were dreadful – you had to pull the starter up from inside and they had solid tyres. He wasn't the only baker – there was Brickenshaws, who had the shop in the Pound, and then there was Deadman's up in the Dean.

Kate Swan, born 1911.

Deadman's pit

My great grandfather William Deadman ran the post office stores in Cookham Dean in the late 1800s. He was also a grocer, corn dealer and baker, and the old bakehouse is still there in the little lane behind. Later on Easts ran a coal yard on the land next to it. When I went to school (Cookham Dean Primary school in the 1940s) there was a big pit close by which was called Deadman's Pit. It was a Victorian rubbish tip full of all sorts of interesting things. Grandfather William Taylor Deadman had Carmonta built in the mid-twenties and ran a bakery there until he retired. The land was an orchard before then. My father also worked there most of his working life. The first paid job I ever had was to clean out and oil the bread tins after school. I was paid ten shillings a week (this was in the late 1940s). There were two big bread ovens, coke fired, and when the bread was baked it was tipped out and put on a rack, which was put outside. I also had to rake out all the ashes from the previous days fire and re-lay the fire, ready for them to start work at four o'clock the next morning. William Meade and Bill Sexton also worked there, they were the other two bakers. Father had to deliver the bread when he'd finished baking. Sometimes it was dark before he'd finished. As Cookham Dean was such a spread out area we had two vans. The shop at the front of the bake house was also a general stores, as well as selling the bread, rolls, cakes and hot cross buns. My father made super wedding and fancy cakes to order. At Christmas time a lot of the houses round here used to bring their turkeys to be cooked in the bread ovens in my Grandfathers time. It was difficult for my father when I went to do my National Service to continue with the deliveries. It was also the time when small bakeries were going out of fashion, sliced wrapped bread was coming in and people forsook all the little local bakeries.

Tony Deadman, born 1936.

Milkman Ernie

My first job in Cookham was doing four months on the milk round. If you want to know a village – be a milkman. In those days it was delivered in cans – there were pint, half pint and quart cans with W. Tuck on the label. We had half a dozen boys to give a hand first thing in the morning. We'd start at six o'clock to take it round to the houses. The bottling up was done in Station Road in the old days and we'd take the cans out on the first round. On the second round we'd

pick up the cans and get ready for the next round. The milk was about 4d a pint. The milk came from Pound Farm which was Randall's farm in those days. They were milking fifty or sixty cows twice a day. As they were milked we'd put it through the cooler and that was it. There was no fancy treatment in those days. Pound Farm was at the end of Terry's Lane and Mr Randall lived there. The cows would graze where the golf course is now. Ernie Tuck and his father had a horse drawn truck, and the dairy was where Vicki Bonds shop is now. They had a good round; every Sunday the Bel and Dragon would have two gallons of cream and in the summertime four or five gallons of milk would be needed every weekend at Cookham Lock, where they would run teas.

Eddie Smyth, born 1909.

Milkman Ernie Tuck with his bike.

Working on the river

My grandfather was a ferryman for forty-five years at Cookham Ferry. In 1929 he retired and my father took over. They were both called John Brooks and both known as Jack. There were three ferries: the Cookham ferry took people across the river onto Sashes Island, from there they walked down to Cookham Lock to the middle ferry, a punt, which took them across to underneath Cliveden Woods, they then walked down to My Lady ferry which took them back over to the Berkshire side near Mill Lane and walked back up to Cookham Village. It was very busy, you used to get all these hiking parties doing the three ferries walk. The Cookham ferry was particularly busy taking people to Sashes Island where they used to pick up the Salters Steamers at Cookham Lock. My father worked from sunrise to sunset, summer and winter. Sometimes on an Ascot Sunday he would take about six hundred people across the river. In the winter he used to get lots of fishermen, it was always busy. There was a special horse-barge to take the horse ferry across. Both boats were kept by the ferryman's cottage, at Cookham Bridge, which went with the job. The Thames Conservancy provided a uniform of a waistcoat, cap and reefer jacket. It was only a penny to go across the ferry, which was a big skiff and could carry eighteen people and himself. He worked in all weathers, although not many people wanted to go across during the floods – he did, though, because he kept his chickens on Sashes Island and he had to go and feed them! My father was the last ferryman at Cookham and the ferry was closed in 1956. Many local people worked for the boatyards: Turks Boatyard at Cookham, Andrews at Bourne End, Townsends just above Bourne End Bridge and Woottens. The Odney Club had their own boats and boatmen down there. I was apprenticed up at Woottens. I earned 10/- a week. We used mahogany mostly and would build a boat by hand from start to finish. We built punts and motor launches but our main thing was sailing dinghies. Most of the well to do families had a boat on the river.

John Brooks, born 1923.

Jack Brooks Snr on the Cookham ferry, 1922.

Cookham Upper ferry in the 1920s.

The start of Odney pottery

I went down to Odney one day and saw these men knocking this old farm building about and I went and had a word with them, and it turned out to be John Bew. He and his wife Grace, who was a weaver, were both Quakers. I got a grant to train as a potter from the Naval Association. I learnt at Odney and also I went up to the Slade for a while. At first we would sell our pots to small craft shops. I have gone round the Lake District with John with a pack on my back selling £80 worth here and there to small shops. It was my job to find the clay for the pots. It all had to be dug up – it was very hard work. One of the other potters was Frank Spindler, George Boddy was the office boy who did a bit of

pottery. We made beer mugs, baskets, plaques, tea pots, vases – all sorts of things. I made lustre ware that went to a little shop in London. I used to make the lustre ware on my own. The colours would depend on what sort of wood you put in the kiln – oak, elm, even local willow off the common. It was a very special place to work.

Leslie Knight, born 1923.

The potter

The Pottery at Odney was set up by John Bew, who ran it until his death in 1953. The John Lewis Partnership brought him to Cookham on the basis that he would show the Partners, when they came to visit the

Leslie Knight (left) with John Bew sitting on the step at Odney Pottery, c. 1950.

slip and squeezed it so that you got a wavy line going round it – a bit like a piping bag. That was peculiar to Odney Pottery. Another characteristic of the pottery was that the slips came through the glaze and made a speckled effect. Underlying patterns could just be scratched on by hand beforehand.

Geoffrey Eastop, born 1921.

Firing the mural

After the war we did a mural – something new which hadn't been done before. It was about fifteen foot square – and the idea was to do John Dory fish on tiles, and the tiles were all made like a picture. You had weed going down, green done in slipware. Frank Spindler worked most of it out, but it was a major job and was a years work for us all. John Bew, the head potter, was very worried about it. It had to be fired in two kilns and we used to take turns on firing it. On the night it was going for the final firing I was watching it all night. I started at seven o'clock in the morning and the firing went on all night through till about one o'clock the next day.

club, how pots were made. It was there initially for educational purposes. He had altruistic ideas, it wasn't there to make a lot of profit for the company. The pottery made at Odney was brown slipware. The technique was as follows: you threw a pot in which ever clay (there were two kinds of clay) and then you got a brush and you dipped it into slip of one colour or another, and while the pot was spinning on the wheel slowly you just run the brush up it so you covered it in the background slip, and then you took a little trailing bag (this was Frank Spindler's idea – he had been brought up in a bakers shop in Bourne End, in fact he would swim to work at the pottery in the river from Bourne End) of

Geoffrey Eastop in his Newbury studio.

Odney jugs.

The mural was absolutely perfect when it came out of the kiln.

Leslie Knight, born 1923.

The pottery closes

John Bew's death bought about a crisis as the John Lewis Partnership wanted the pottery to make more profit. They brought in a new designer to use a new technique and bring in industrial methods. The Odney Pottery works was not really suitable for this and was closed in the autumn of 1954.

Geoffrey Eastop, born 1921.

Building a business

Father set up his building business in the late 1930s. He used to do maintenance at Cliveden and over the years he got to know the Astor family. At one time they wanted a lift put in because the old Lord Astor was getting elderly, and my father had the job of cutting right through Cliveden House to put the lift shaft down. One of the walls was fourteen foot thick. There was a figure of Mercury on the top of the clock tower, which came crashing down during a storm in the 1950s. They salvaged all the pieces and had a replica cast which had to be hoisted back up on a block and tackle. It was then painted in gold paint. When the clock tower was renovated again recently it was taken down and hasn't been replaced. I also remember immediately after the Second World War, he built council houses for Cookham Rural District Council – Hillcrest Avenue and Whyteladyes Lane. That was a big contract.

Keith and Barry Hatch,
born 1932 and 1935.

Brick kiln

I had one year at the Brick Kiln at Pinkneys Green in 1961 – they closed down about three years later. They didn't make bricks then – they made tiles and Keyter clads, hanging tiles of all different shapes. They made beautiful ornaments and gargoyles before the war. There were big ovens, kilns – which during the war were used as billets for the Army. On the right-hand side they had new round kilns and the clay was dug out on the other side and taken across. The clay was taken from all the big holes that you can still see around the Malders Lane area. They had a big bucket on a cable that used to go up to the Pug House and would be tipped down to go through the pugging machines. That was where the clay was worked until it was plyable. Then the big blocks were taken to the tile machine and they went through like a big mincer with the shape of the tiles they wanted to make. They would come off and be put in the dryer then brought back after a couple of weeks when they were dry, and then they were baked in the oven. When I was there they were using the round kilns, not the big old ones any more. Some tiles were made by hand. You had a mould, pressed the studs in, would tip them out and let them dry. There was a gang of people doing it. There was a West Indian guy called Charlie who you couldn't beat. He'd sing and dance about in his big wellies working faster than anyone and be pushing these things along. It was really nice working with the West Indians who had just come over to this country. There were waterholes everywhere to get the water to puddle the clay. There were two or three lovely big steam traction engines to transport the tiles away. They looked wonderful with two or three trailers when they were going to London.

Ray Nash, born 1929.

Painting gigs and carts

My dad was partner in the garage (opposite the post office) in Cookham Rise. He used to paint the cars. He was apprenticed there when he left school and everything was hand painted, the gigs and carriages. He used to do Governor's Carts and prams for Lord Astor, and he did all the lining. It gradually grew up and he got round to cars. He was born in Cookham down the village, in 1888 in Cornberrow Cotte. His name was Frederick Alfred Robinson. His father was a builder, I think. His initials are inside Seaton Cottage (Station Hill) somewhere. My Mum was in service locally. They met at a flower show in Moor Hall and they got married in 1910. Dad got some money from the Widbrook Fund for his tools. When he came back from the First World War he went back there, and I know he was varnishing by hand. We didn't dare breathe because if we raised any dust it would make a mark.

Lucy Edwards, born 1914.

Hard work

My Gran, Fanny, used to work really hard. I remember her always doing washing and ironing in Apsley Cottages. She got up at four o'clock in the morning to light the copper and used an old flat iron. Women did work really hard. She was often still working until ten o'clock at night. My grandfather won the Croix de Guerre in the Great War, and when he came back he was a gardener and did some building. We don't know why he got the medal, but he was as hard as nails. In the last war he joined the police and stayed with them until he died in 1948. He got into a fight in Maidenhead with some Canadians when he was on duty and that more or less finished him off. His real name was Walter Steven, but everyone knew him

At the brick kilns, c. 1930.

The derelict brick works in 1975.

as 'Darky' Fenner. My grandad's sister married Teddy Wakeling – everyone knew him!

Ray Fenner, born 1935.

Moor Hall

I came to Cookham in 1954 working for the company which became ICL. I was sent to Moor Hall as the first lecturer in punch card machines. It was still reminiscent of what it did in the war – when the animators were there. There was a wonderful lady there called 'Sally' (Freda) Salberg. She stayed on as housekeeper after J. Arthur Rank had gone. I used to tell her she was the best Christian Jew that I knew. She was baptized and confirmed in my time there. We had a wonderful gardener there called Reg Ireson, who was a fantastic gardener. He and Sally used to win all the prizes for everything – particularly the sweet peas. Reg and a whole group of us dug out and built a cricket pitch at Moor Hall. Where the beautiful new extension is at the back, below the Ha Ha, there were four or five green huts which were the old dormitories. My son, many years later, helped to convert one into the pavilion at Cookham Dean Cricket Club. I met my wife Margaret at Moor Hall – she was on a course and sleeping in one of the huts in the grounds.

Rick Terry

Time of your life

I worked at Moor Hall for twenty-nine years, doing everything. I worked down the men's dormitories. You had the time of your life down there! They were wooden huts round the back. There were twenty-four men's rooms, two to a room, and more for the girls. They had a cinema there where we would watch the films they had made there. It was all cartoons. They made Robin Hood there. A lot of the fellows who had come out of the forces used to come there. Bob Monkhouse was an animator there once.

Connie Fenner, born 1910.

Death duties

My old gran used to lay the bodies out. If somebody died in the village they'd send for

On an ICL course at Moor Hall in the 1970s.

Gran. I'd go with her sometime to help turn the bodies over. She used to wash them, and put cotton wool in their cheeks. They always knew where she was going because she had an old sit-up-and-beg bike and this big carrier bag in the front with scissors and cotton wool and sheets and stuff. She never charged anybody. She would lay them out and then they'd go in a coffin and be put on the table in the front room. They'd stop in there for a couple of days until they went up to the church. Everybody would pull their curtains.

Ray Fenner, born 1935.

The toll gate

I went to work at Jackson's paper mill in Bourne End where I stayed for seventeen years. I used to cycle to work along Ferry Lane in snow, ice, fog, all sorts of weather. We had to go through the toll gate, so I had to pay a penny every time I went to work or came home. There weren't many cars around – so it was quite safe. I remember the first time I saw a car in Cookham Dean. It was wonderful, they would go up and down the road from the big houses.

Nancy Harvey, born 1916.

Coke on the causeway

Old Grandad Wicks had horses and contracted for the old Berkshire Council, mending the roads. He had a horse that would pull the tar pot while the lorry would dump the shingle. He had two sentry boxes, like the ones at Windsor Castle, that he kept in the orchard. Every October, to be ready for the floods, they'd go down to the Moor and the men who made the roads would lay five cwt of coke on the Causeway, putting a sentry box at either end operating a stop-go system.

Ray Nash, born 1929.

Tar on the road

As a child I would watch them tar the road in Cookham High Street and would always get covered in tar. When you spray the road with tar you have a tar-making machine with a fire underneath and you melt the tar. There was a pump on top that would pump the red-hot tar out, and then men would hold sprays and spray the road. A horse and cart would come along with more chippings and spread them on top, then the steamroller would roll it in. There were little puddles of tar all along the side of the road, and we kids would go and play in it. My knees used to get cleaned up with petrol from the garage! Men would wrap paper bags round their legs to stop getting burned and tarred. Their boots would be solid with tar. They would wrap things round their necks and everywhere.

Peter Remington, born 1922.

The chimney sweep

Mr Skinner was the chimney sweep. I think he acted as the sexton at the church as well, digging the graves. He would walk round, or go on his bike, with all his brooms and brushes. They used to make a terrible mess. He was a very short man with a moustache. His eyebrows were always full of soot.

Ray Lewington, born 1939.

The opera singer

One of my Aunts, Nellie Marina, had embarked on a career as a singer at the time of the Great War. She was a soprano with the Covent Garden Opera Company. She took the stage name Sheila Gray, which was her mother's maiden name. I clearly remember the family gathered round a radio listening to a broadcast from London. Granny was sure

Opera singer Nellie Marina Hatch.

The fire chief

My father was the fire chief at Cookham. He took over when Skipper Hatch retired. He'd joined the fire brigade when he was eighteen. When he came back after the war he re-started it because it had been disbanded. I was about ten and we were the only people with a telephone. If there was a fire during the night I had to get up and call two or three of the men who lived within running distance – see me running up the road and they'd tear down the road on their bikes. I remember when Formosa caught fire down Mill Lane. They couldn't get at it because of the floods. During the Second World War they were on standby to go to Coventry. They never went, but they were ready if called. He got a medal for long service.

Lucy Edwards, born 1914.

The coal merchant

Our grandfather Jobey Hatch died delivering a sack of coal to Odney Club. He was the local coal merchant and my uncle Arthur (his eldest son) used to work with him. My father continued the business all through the war and into the early sixties, running it alongside his building firm. It was quite a big operation, they rented a siding at Cookham Station and the coal came in open-sided wagons mainly from Wales, all the different grades of coal. It would be shovelled into 100 cwt bags loaded onto a lorry and taken round the village. Some people paid the driver as he put the coal in their coal-sheds, others had a monthly account. If the trucks had to go back it was stored in pens at the station. They had a little tin hut as an office. Jim East was the other coal merchant in the village at the time.

Keith and Barry Hatch,
born 1932 and 1935.

she could distinguish Nell's voice. I remember her singing really loud in church, and wishing that she wouldn't!

John Field, born 1924.

The stationmaster

When my husband came to Cookham to live he didn't have a job – so Mr Pine the Stationmaster asked him, because of his railway experience, if he wanted to do some temporary work as a porter. He took it because he was fed up with not having any work. He went from porter to Stationmaster. We were offered the cottage at the station, but it wasn't as modern as our place in Hillcrest Avenue, so we didn't take it. You had to walk across the yard to get from the housing side to the kitchen, so if you wanted to wash up or anything you had a nice little walk!

Joan Stringer, born 1922.

Soft hands!

My grandfather died when I was sixteen so I remember the coal yard well. He shared it with Mr East, who was the coal merchant who did the Dean. At first they used a horse and cart, but my Grandfather was the first one to use a lorry, which he drove with my uncle. He never looked terribly dirty, and I can always remember him coming home and putting lard on his hands. Then he would wash them and all the coal would come off and he had lovely soft hands. You would have thought they would be harsh, but they never were.

Joan Stringer, born 1922.

Working locally

My parents came to Cookham for work. Mother was a housekeeper at the cottage round by the church, and my father a gardener. The gentleman next door, Mr Gould, was a cabinet maker, the lady next door on the other side was a dressmaker, four doors down there was a haberdashers in the sitting room and most people were gardeners or worked for the builders. One was a chauffeur for Katy Bird.

Nancy James, born 1927.

Blowing the hooter

My family arrived in 1933 when my father came from Croydon to be the chauffeur for Mr Joe Allen at Dial close. We lived in the chauffeur's cottage. We never knew when he would be coming home, but I do remember when he drove out in the Roller, if he was not coming home that day he would give two blows on the hooter. If he didn't blow the horn we could expect him back! He was never allowed to walk round the front of the car. He always had to go round the back to open the doors for passengers. We always used to have to doff our caps if we saw the family.

John Webb, born 1928.

Butler at The Grange

I was born in Ross Cottage, Graham Road. My father, William Gant, was in service when they married. After they married they moved to Hamfield Cottages and eventually he became the butler at The Grange. His employer was Mrs Balfour-Allan. There was a full staff there, and the chauffeur slept on the premises to look after the car. Dad worked all hours and would often come home really late if they had a party. He had to stop and see that everything had to be locked up. He must have started there in 1923, and worked there until John Lewis's bought the house. There was a head gardener and three other gardeners, and they kept a beautiful garden. The pears were all trained over hoops to make an arch. Dad would wear morning trousers, and had to get dressed up to the nines for parties.

Joan Stringer, born 1922.

The parlour maid

I came to Cookham Dean in the 1930s to work as parlour maid at Harwood House. You did everything in the dining room, clean the silver, lay the table, wait at the table and all that sort of thing. You'd look after the young gentlemen when they came, and press their clothes and everything. I had two rooms to do. There were four maids at Harwood, and my job was to keep the dining room clean, and also the big sitting room and the lounge. You didn't have hoovers, you'd use a brush. I had a uniform, a red dress and a white frilly apron, white cap and white sleeves, and it was made by a lady in Cookham Dean. You'd change at lunchtime. I had a print cotton frock in the morning, and at about half past twelve I was allowed half an hour to change. In that half an hour the housemaid took over to answer the door or the telephone while I went and changed. I had my own bedroom right at the top. You could look over and see Windsor Castle. It was lovely. I met my husband at Harwood. His father, Frederick William Dyer, was head gardener at Harwood, and he lived at Harwood Lodge with his son Fred. Downstairs was the lounge, the hall where the front door was, the morning room and there was a conservatory but Mrs Martin Bird had that taken down and made a very long drawing room. Then there was a dining room, a serving room for the dining room and a parlour maid's room that led into the kitchen. All the silver and the china for the tea was in the parlour maids room. In the kitchen there was a big range and on one side was the maids sitting room, and the other the scullery where the pots were washed. We had quite a bit of time off in the sitting room, and it faced the front door so you could see who was coming before they rang the doorbell.

Dora Dyer, born 1907.

Jobs for locals

Mrs Martin Bird lived in Harwood House, and in the 1920s, during the General Strike, she made work for the local men by employing them as gardeners. In the depression most people found local work of some kind. My mother came from Ross on Wye to go into service there. She enjoyed it even though she was the scullery maid. My father was the jobbing gardener there –

which was how they met. They married and bought a house in Dean Lane, which was a grocery shop. My mother looked after the shop and my dad worked on the land.

Pat Woodbridge, born 1927.

Carpenters apprentice

My grandfather lived in Ventnor Cottages. He worked for Copas on the farm. If you worked for them just before the war you had 28s a week. If you worked for Frost's, which my father eventually did, you got 30s. In the building trade, when I started as a carpenter, you got 1s 6d an hour. We were much better off because I got £3 10s a week. Father had to pay £30 for me to be an apprentice. I went as a carpenters apprentice at Hardings. At the time there wasn't a house in Cookham Dean that Hardings hadn't built or I hadn't worked in!

John Taft, born 1921.

The church clock at Cookham Dean

I was a carpenter for Hardings. I did a five year apprenticeship, and then had to do another year as 'an improver'. One of the things I built was a case for the clock in Cookham Dean church. I remember the man came down from Birmingham with the clock mechanism. 'Bomber' Harris had to dig a pit for the pendulum to swing in, and I remember 'Snowy' Copas helping as well. The man said the clock was accurate within two seconds a month. We had a new bell as well, and I recall the vicar asking what note it struck. He went to the organ and played a 'D' – and that was right!

John Webb, born 1928.

7 Planting and Ploughing

The last farmer at Oveys

My Grandfather George had Oveys farm in Cookham High Street, which was a working farm until he died in 1915. Father could have come out of the army being a farmer's son and taken it on, but he thought there was more to life in butchering than there was in farming, so he became a butcher. After he died my grandmother sold up and moved to Wistaria Cottage. That was the end of Oveys as a farm. There was never a lot of land with the farm, it was all rented pasture and common land. My Uncle Bill was a horticulturalist at Widbrook Nurseries, which is now where Sutton Close is. The whole of the area is now covered in new housing. He lived at the Nurseries with his wife Rosina in a large wooden, clapboard bungalow. He entered lots of shows and won many prizes.

James Hatch, born 1930.

Working at Harwood

They had a very good cook at Harwood in Cookham Dean, and Mrs Martin Bird entertained quite a lot at weekends, particularly when her boys were home. There were four maids and a cook living in, and a chauffeur who lived in a flat over the stables. There were five gardeners. There were terraces to the front of the house and beyond the garages there was a chicken run, where Little Harwood has now been built. They had

rockeries and five or six greenhouses. My father-in-law Fred William Dyer was head gardener. You would see him in the vinery with the scissors thinning out the grapes. They would go on the table for dessert. His wife used to make wine with what was left. He was a great one for showing. The kitchen garden was up on the right of the road. He came to Cookham Dean in 1910. He worked at Harwood for more than forty years before he died. When I married his son I gave up work and we lived in one of Pudsey Cottages while Fred, my husband, carried on at Harwood as a gardener.

Dora Dyer, born 1907.

Father was an under-gardener

My grandfather came from Wiltshire in about 1880 to be head gardener for the Ellis family at Bigfrith House. He lived in the little bungalow next door. When the Ellis family then moved to Winter Hill House my grandfather Albert moved into the gardener's cottage up there. The house called 'Back of Beyond' was built where the vegetable garden used to be. My grandmother Louise acted as a housekeeper for the Ellis's. My father became an under-gardener there when he was fifteen. He'd gone down to the Cookham Rise Senior School very soon after it opened. There were magnificent rock gardens and ponds at Winter Hill House in those days. Waterers, the nursery people, used to use the pictures of

Fred William Dyer in the vinery at Harwood House, 1930s.

the gardens in their catalogues. There were something like five long greenhouses, twenty metres long, and there was a peach house, and a nectarine house. They were heated by little stoves, so grandfather or father would have to go back in the evening to stoke the boiler up, and go back early morning to stoke it again. It was a life of dedication. I can remember them going back in the middle of the night if there was a frost to make sure the boiler was still working. Father worked until he was eighty.

Ray Lewington, born 1939.

Gardening at The Mount

I started work at The Mount when I was fifteen in about 1953. I earned thirty shillings a week and when I became twenty-one they put it up to £3 10s a week. There were five full-time gardeners there then and a cook and caretaker. The family only came to The Mount at weekends because they had a house in London that they lived in during the week. Every weekend we had to get flowers for the house and have all their vegetables ready. The gardens of about six acres were absolutely beautiful, they were kept immaculate. There was an enormous rockery which came down all through the Harwood House side, it went under the road and into The Mount. The spring provided waterfalls that were running all the time. We had to clean it out every year and put lime all around the sides. There were five enormous ponds, all fed by that spring. The vegetable garden used to supply about three shops in Maidenhead, and then we had to box up vegetables and send them to London for the family and all their daughters and sons each week. I used to take fruit up to

Harwood House. We grew nectarines, peaches and apricots – they were enormous green houses. We used to have to keep all the boilers going in the greenhouses, they had to be filled up with coke every morning in the winter. The head gardener used to do all the shows including the one that was held in Dean Meadow. I was there for the Coronation and they gave us a painting of the Queen and £20 each, which was a lot of money then.

Ron Haines, born 1937.

The Cookham Dean bean

Mr Joe Tomlin was a gardener for Lady Beechcroft at Little Mount and he was an excellent gardener. He saved the best seeds from year after year and he perfected his bean. He marketed it through Carters, and got hardly any money from them. There are better beans now, but they were very, very large and good croppers. My father grew some of the Cookham Dean beans and entered them for a *Daily Mail* competition in 1937. I made him a box that was eighteen inches long for them – but it was too short. He won third prize of £5 and spent 30s of it on a striking clock.

John Taft, born 1921.

Coombe End House

My husband Fred became gardener at Coombe End House. We lived in the cottage next to the house. We had three bedrooms and a bathroom and we were facing the Common. The other side of us was a big

Carter's Catalogue entry for the Cookham Dean Bean.

garage. Mrs Manners-Wood was a widow, and her son Peter lived in a house very near called Limberlost, which has now changed it's name. She had two old ladies as staff. They never went out anywhere and were totally devoted to her. The one was eighty when she died. I would go in and help out a bit too. It was after the war, and things had really changed. She only had Fred as a gardener, and another one that came a couple of days a week. He only had one little greenhouse there, but was fully employed on the rest of the garden. There were lots and lots of roses and dahlias. He worked there until he retired in 1979. Mrs Manners-Wood was over ninety when she stopped driving her car, and everyone would give her a wide berth when she went to the shop. Her car was always more than half over the road.

Dora Dyer, born 1907.

Everyone helped with cherry picking

Most people were employed in farming, gardening or by the builders, Hardings and Colin Hatch. Then Jacksons opened the paper mill at Bourne End and they were paying twice as much, so some started to go over there on shift work. Everybody helped out with the cherry picking – I remember coming home from school as a twelve year old and going cherry picking. The men would be up the trees, and if a branch needed pruning they'd cut it off and give it to us lads to get the cherries and put them in to chips. They were raffia baskets with a metal handle. When it came to my turn to get a job there was a change across the country, and Mr Ellis, who my father worked for as a gardener, got me to go to the Electricity Board and I got an apprenticeship.

Ray Lewington, born 1939.

Bigfrith Farm.

Harry Parsons of Bigfrith Farm and his working horses.

Bigfrith Farm

Bigfrith Farm was sold off from the Bisham Estate to my Grandfather Henry Parsons (they used to call him Harry) in 1919. He was already the tenant and he and my grandmother lived across the road in Bigfrith Cottage. There was fourteen acres of land but they rented more. They rented around by the Hockett and the only house in those days was Hockett Corner, where Revd Thicke lived at one time. There was no water on and so they ran a pipe up to Hockett Cottage and bought the supply across. It's still the same supply now. They used to grow cereals and fruit, and some of the tall cherry trees are still here. There was a ladder house (which still exists), a wooden building of about fifty-four feet long, which stored the long ladders that were

needed to pick the walnuts and cherries. The ladders were made locally by Hardings. They also had fattening cattle, which they grazed on Cockmarsh. My grandparents had three children, my Uncle Harry, my mother Edith (who they always called Queenie) and another daughter. Harry trained to be a baker but he was brought back here to work on the land when they bought this place. I don't think he was very pleased about that. Mother used to help on the farm, taking the fruit down to Cookham station on the horse and cart and that used to go up to London, to Covent Garden. They also used to supply to local greengrocers. In the 1930s when they weren't making much money and times were difficult they sold some of the land off to Mrs Manners Wood who lived at Coombe End. Some of the houses on the other side of

Lot 12.

(Coloured *Yellow* on Plan).

The Very Desirable

Freehold Small Holding

situated at Bigfrith, Cookham Dean, and known as

"Bigfrith Farm,"

consisting of

Brick, Timber and Tile Cottage

containing 2 Living Rooms, Scullery, Larder, and 3 Bedrooms,

Brick and Tile Cottage

containing Living Room, Scullery, and 2 Bedrooms.

The Outbuildings

comprise 2 Barns, Stable, Cattle Shed, Wood Shed, and Ladder House, and Cart Shed with Loft over, and

14 Acres of Highly Productive

Market Garden Land

as set out in the

SCHEDULE.

No. on Plan.	Description.					Area.
217	Orchard	...	...	...	...	˙176
219	Ditto	...	...	...	...	1˙672
220	House, Paddock and Buildings	...	...	...	...	˙400
221	Arable	...	...	...	...	4˙754
222	Orchard	...	...	...	...	˙510
264	Ditto	...	...	...	...	˙580
265	Cottage, Garden and Buildings	...	...	...	...	˙270
267	Arable	...	...	...	...	6˙390
					Total	14˙752

In the occupation of Mr. Henry Parsons with other lands on Lease for 14 years from the 29th day of September, 1910.

Apportioned Rent **£30** per annum.

The Vicarial Tithe commuted at £1 8s. 0d.

Sales details of Bigfrith Farm in 1919.

Bigfrith Lane were built on it. They also rented some of it back at some stage. My Uncle Harry spent all his life working here until he died in 1956 and then the farm was handed over to my mother. It wasn't making much money; times were changing. I trained as a plumber when I left school, because someone had to bring in the money. The cottage must be one of the oldest in Cookham Dean, as some of the walls are wattle and daub.

David Wiggins, born 1940.

Helping out

During the Second World War I was a conscientious objector. It was a very big decision and I just had to be one in the end. On the whole the local people were terribly good about it. I decided I must help to keep things going so I opted for working on the land and I came out to Cookham Dean to farm and was farming for Jim Ricketts. Cookham Dean was a mass of cherry orchards, and people used to come out from London to see the blossom in springtime and the colour in the autumn. I worked long long hours with the farm workers doing everything they did. At cherry harvesting time we'd be out at five o'clock in the morning picking cherries (Black Eagle, White Heart, Acasha – a cooking cherry) then at ten o'clock the lorry would come along and collect all the baskets of cherries we'd picked and run them off to market. We'd then go for breakfast.

Ralph Thompson, born 1913.

Working on the Copas farms

My father was a farm worker at Kings Coppice Farm. He actually started work at the Chequers public house in 1902 when he was ten, and that was then tenanted by the Copas family. I think he called himself 'back door boy', but I don't know what that meant. As the Copas family got more into farming there was more scope to go into farm working and he moved to Kings Coppice farm. The cottage is still there and I was born there, and he worked for the Copas family for seventy-seven years – he was the longest-serving farm worker in England. In their heyday the Copas Farms employed a lot of people and there were a lot of horses used. Lea Farm was the old stables for about three pairs of horses who were working nearly everyday. The corn was cut by binder there were no combines, tractors you stood up on, it was just an old-fashioned way of working. I started working for Copas Farms in 1946. I worked there for sixteen years, the best years of my life. I enjoyed every minute of it. You had to turn your hand to anything. Sometimes we started at seven o'clock in the morning, out in all weathers tractor driving with only an ex-government surplus army greatcoat to keep you warm. The whole of Kings Coppice valley was just fruit trees; cherries, apples and pears. People used to come in the spring just to see the blossoms, on a Thursday when it was half day closing in Maidenhead the bus used to be full of people coming to see the blossoms in Cookham Dean. Virtually every working man in Cookham Dean spent some time of his life picking fruit because it was extra money; it was all evening work and piece work, they got paid so much per container (chips, we used to call the baskets) of fruit. There was an awful lot of cherries to pick you see, there were some big trees and big ladders required. In the early days it used to go to Cookham station by horse and van and then on a truck to the London markets, but latter years, after the war in 1946, it was transported by lorry. As soon as I got my driving licence that was one of my jobs to go to the London fruit markets every other night.

Gordon Harris, born 1932.

Lea Farm.

'Fuzzy' Godfrey

Old Fuzzy Godfrey lived up the top; he was like everybody then, you did what you could to get a shilling. He was a tree lopper, without using a chain saw... anybody who had an elm tree and there were a lot round then, he'd take the top out for them. He'd stand on his head when he cut the bow off, if there was a prong on it and he would sing out 'cuckoo!' and everybody thought they'd heard the cuckoo! He made baskets from osiers (willow) gathered by donkey from Longridge and Temple. The osiers would be soaked in the little ponds that were around the area to keep them pliable before weaving. It was pretty horrible work in cold weather. Fuzzy had a few sheds down the Hockett where he'd make his fruit baskets and keep his pigs. Up in Cookham Dean they were all basket makers, Fitchett and Parsons were another two who made cherry sieves for Walter Frost who used to keep them in work.

Ray Nash, born 1929.

Walnut bashing

Cookhan Dean was famous for it's walnut trees and when I was working on the land during the war we'd go walnut bashing with enormous ladders which had a wide splayed foot and could be as much as forty foot high. Jim Ricketts was amazing at handling these things, it was a real skill. You stand them on one foot and handle them from one side only, pivoting on that point, then you balance your weight against them and swing them over to another point. You would go up the ladder stick one leg through a rung to secure yourself and then wave sticks around in order to bash the walnuts, which would then fall to the ground ready to be picked up. Those were the days almost before tractors and we had a horse who did a lot of the work at harvest time and one little tractor. Some produce went on the train up to London and some went to wholesalers in Maidenhead.

Ralph Thompson, born 1913.

Grandfather was the bailiff

My grandparents were born in Cherry Tree Cottage on the Cricket Common in Cookham Dean and I lived with them when I was small. It was a lovely cottage. My grandfather was the bailiff for Walter Frost who owned lots of land and cherry orchards round there. Mr Frost lived in Ridgemount. My grandfather managed the plantations – there were seven of them. One of them, where the new part of the school is built, was Godfrey's, which belonged to Walter Frost. There were cherry trees, plum trees, currants and gooseberries. There was a big barn in there. Behind Cherry Tree Cottage was another orchard, mainly apple trees, and then there was Hardings, which was damsons and plums, and Reddings which was another apple orchard. They had four regular staff all year round, and then in the summer the casual staff would come in. They would be local people, and there was never any shortage. The housewives would come in picking the low stuff, the currants and gooseberries. We're talking about in the 1930s. Dave Hatch who lived in Cookham Dean Bottom was the carter, and he'd come and collect the fruit and take it down to the station. Right by the side of Cherry Tree Cottage were some barns and stables, and the cart was kept up there. Mr Parsons the basket weaver would sit outside the stables on the common weaving away. He worked piece work – and he was always busy. He used to soak the canes in a long trough and was a real master at his craft. He would make bushels and half bushels, and he'd also make the kips for taking up the ladders. They were long thin baskets with a hook and a rope that you hauled up the ladder, then hooked on while you filled it. I called them 'kipses' – but I don't know what the real name was.

Pat Woodbridge, born 1927.

Rearing pheasants

When I was eight or nine I loved working with Grandad Wicks on the farm, when they were rearing pheasants. I used to go over there with him, he'd set the men working, they'd fill the water barrel up on wheels and harness it to one of the old horses who wouldn't run away, and I'd take it up to the Long Walk (towards Pinkney's Green, by the Golden Ball pub). The first thing I would do would be back the water barrel in, pull the plug out and release the water for the pheasants. Then I'd go into Mr Taylor, the keeper's hut and get some eggs for my breakfast. They hung red lanterns all across the fields to stop the foxes, although there weren't many around. In about March me and Mrs Taylor would take biscuit tins with gravel in and flush out the foxes – they didn't live too long then!

Ray Nash, born 1929.

8 Fun and Games

Plenty to do

We always seemed to have plenty to do. Everybody congregated on the moor to play rounders or something, or to watch them play football. In the street we could play marbles or hoops because there wasn't the traffic then. At flood times we would put a peg on the water line and then rush out the next morning to see if it had risen or gone down at all. All our spare time was spent either in or on the river. We had 6d a week pocket money, my brother and I, and we used to go to see Mr Turk (at the boatyard) and he would let us have a boat for the whole afternoon. We would often go down to Odney for a swim.

Kate Swan, born 1911.

Hundreds of swimmers

I'll never forget when I first went to Odney. I got the shock of my life because there were hundreds and hundreds of people down there. They would come from all over the place on their bikes. There was a café down there at one time, but the war almost finished

Cookham Deaners on a day out in the 1920s.

that because of the rationing. Even after the war hundreds of people came from London and would camp out.

Connie Fenner, born 1910.

The 'beanfeasters'

It used to be about 2s 6d return fare on the train to London and the 'beanfeasters' used to come down to Odney Common and picnic and run races and things. A big party would come, all sorts of people, bringing all their own food and playing rounders. My father taught loads of local children to swim with a pole with a belt on the end, and Mr Edward Cooper ran a gym club for boys and girls of the village. Pryce-Jones (the chemist) used to go to Odney every morning in his pyjamas to swim.

Kate Swan, born 1911.

Girls tied to the bridge!

I remember one year coming in to Cookham to watch the regatta – in those days all of Cookham Bridge was decorated with lanterns and all the other side of the river was lit up. There were roundabouts at John Turk's boathouse, there would be a fair in the meadows and on the moor. I used to take part in the rag regatta at Odney, which was organized by John Lewis. We'd have girls tied to the bridge and have to paddle up the stream to the Japanese bridge to untie them.

Leslie Knight, born 1923.

River patrol

Odney was a very popular bathing spot and that Whit Monday I remember it was packed. We had a super water polo team and we used to practice down this side of the weir at Odney. We used to take on teams from other

Mr Edward Cooper's Athletic Club in 1920.

places. My wife and her friends were very good swimmers... and I asked her out on a date to Bray bell-ringing. The Rag Regatta in September was fun and games, making people laugh; diving and falling in the river and capsizing punts. Darky Fenner and I patrolled up and down the river in a barge while Ernie Tuck's band played. He had an orchestra who used to do dances in the Athletic Hall at the Crown on Saturday nights.

Eddie Smyth born 1909

We'd walk for miles

As boys we sang in Holy Trinity choir twice on Sundays and Friday nights for practice, the pay was 7s 6d a quarter. Weddings were worth 2s 6d. At other times we used to walk miles and miles going bird nesting, exploring, fishing and we swam in the pools at Odney. We used to go to the cinema in Bourne End on a Saturday afternoon. We would catch the two o'clock train from Cookham and would often walk back over the railway bridge.

Keith Hatch and Barry Hatch,
born 1932 and 1935.

Athletic endeavour

I used to take boys from Cookham Rise Secondary out for a run. We would go two or three miles. Later on I started an athletics club on the recreation ground. We put a five lap running track down, and we had hundreds of children turning up, and not many helpers! It lasted for a couple of years. That was where the football pitch is now. I remember the youth club that would meet at the church hall run by Ben Gunner. This was in the 1960s and they played very loud music.

Stanley Jones, born 1914.

On a rat hunt

On one occasion I was taken out in

Ernie Tuck's River Band.

Cookham Dean to watch a rat hunt. Lots of people with terrier dogs stood round in a circle. Many had rats in baskets which were let out one by one. They then timed with stopwatches to see how long before the rat was killed by a dog. It was country sport, the sort of spectacle that you took a child to. I had a little dinghy on the river which we kept at Woottens Boatyard. My mother and I used to row to Marlow and have tea at a café by the weir. My mother used to row back to Woottens and I would swim all the way alongside the boat. There were some people who lived in Gibraltar Lane who were great friends with my mother. Just before the war they hired a television for the evening and gave a big dinner party to watch the television. I was eight or nine at the time and wore a party dress. None of us had ever seen television before – it was very hazy and quite flickery. It was a really big event.

Esilda Mezulianik, born 1929.

Christmas parties

I was born into the house I still live in on Cookham High Street. I can remember walking under the kitchen table when I was very small, and having lots of Christmas and birthday parties. They would always be in our own homes. We'd play pass the parcel and musical chairs, hunt the thimble, pin the tail on the donkey and all that sort of thing. I had a dolly's pram for Christmas once, and a nice doll my mother had dressed in handmade clothes. We'd have books and bags of sweets. We'd always have a Christmas tree with lights on.

Nancy James, born 1927.

Plays and pantos

The Cookham and Cookham Dean Arts Club was very active when we arrived – they would put on plays and pantos. They were the organization before the Tarrystone Players. Our children were in the pantos. When we first came there were some posters advertising *The Babes of Quarry Woods*, which must have been in 1951. The following year at Christmas they put on *A Midsummer Night's Dream* – which we thought was an interesting choice for Christmas.

Stanley Jones, born 1914.

A Midsummer Night's Dream

Stanley Dangerfield, of Crufts fame, used to live in the village. I was in the Arts group production of *A Midsummer Night's Dream*. My father played the music, and I was chosen to be one of the fairies. Stanley Dangerfield played Thisbe and would collect me from home in his grey Rolls Royce. It was hard to take him seriously when I had seen him on stage in his blonde plaited wig!

Enid Grant (Jenkins), born 1943.

Leading light

Mr Vassall Adams was the leading light at the time and was chairman for the Arts Club, which staged some Cookham pantomimes. He was once seen, never forgotten! His hands were always moving, always gesticulating, and he had a rather high voice. He was an employee of the Ottoman Bank or something and he loved acting and producing. He must have been in his forties when we first met him. It was such a small place Cookham, and we got to know almost all of them to say hello to.

Georgina Jones, born 1917.

A Vassall Adams Production in 1954.

Youth drama

In the 1970s we ran a youth theatre workshop for the Tarrystone Players, of which I was one of the founder members in the mid-sixties. We entered the Maidenhead Drama Festival four years running. The first production was *The Canterville Ghost* and we won the youth trophy. We also entered Cookham Festival which was a biannual festival of the arts – art, poetry, drama and music.

Lynda Whitworth, born 1925.

Adult drama

The Tarrystone Players were formed just after we arrived. Christine Millard was involved with drama mainly with the pantomime and she had a youth group. She eventually decided to form a group called the Tarrystone Players in the early sixties. It grew in strength and they asked me if I were willing to direct productions. I think my first production was *Love In a Mist* and I went on to direct many, many plays for them. I loved productions that had what I call light and shade – comedy, drama and pathos. They went down very well in Cookham.

Ruth Charlton-Brown, born 1916.

Not allowed to dance

We used to have a social at the chapel occasionally. Mother would go and help. I wasn't allowed to go dancing when I got into my teens, mother didn't approve. When I was nine they bought a piano and I was taught to play which I enjoyed. Then Dad took up the flute and we used to play duets and Mum used to sing. We had concerts at the Wesley Hall and I used to accompany them.

Lucy Edwards, born 1914.

Hoops and tops

I was born and brought up in Albion Cottages in Cookham Dean – we'd play in the road for hours with our hoops and tops. We'd mark up the road and play hopscotch right in the road and if we saw a car come we would run and get our note books so we could write down the number and then we'd tell our friends what we'd seen.

Frances Harvey, born 1918.

Leapfrog too close to the church

We would play on the little common outside the church. Father came down from the allotment one day and found us playing leapfrog and he was very cross. He said it wasn't the place to play leapfrog as we were too close to the church. They were very strict in those days. We would play with our skipping ropes in Albion Lane, and we had rubber balls. I was very naughty once I remember. I was sitting on the church wall and the vicar came up and said it wasn't the place to sit on and he told me off.

Nancy Harvey, born 1916.

Leave the street tidy

We would play mostly on the moor in Cookham and out on the pavement. We had our own tree house that we'd made. We'd play hopscotch on the pavement, but we had to rub off the chalk before we went in at night. We weren't allowed to leave the pavement untidy. We used to have skipping ropes and spinning tops. We used to have to take those on The Causeway, we weren't allowed them on the pavement because there were just a few cars around. We were very naughty because when it got time for bed we would run further across the Marsh Meadows so they had a long way to come to look for us!

Nancy James, born 1927.

Not allowed to play

I wasn't allowed to play with the village children, because my parents thought I would pick up a Berkshire accent, so I was always taken out for walks with Nanny. I would be taken fishing with my net and rod, but you didn't mix with the village children. That's the way it was. So you went to a different school.

Peter Remington, born 1922.

The crab-apple tree

As children we would play in Grange Road all the time. Wakelings End wasn't built then – it was Teddy Wakelings smallholding. He'd turn in his grave if he knew it had been sold for housing. There was a crab-apple tree up the road where we always used to play. I remember the first houses being built after the war.

Margaret Tuck, born 1937.

Birds nesting

In the Dean as a boy I remember playing lots of cricket and football and going birds nesting. We used to take the eggs and blow them and we had collections. We'd have one egg for each kind of bird.

Pat Woodbridge, born 1927.

Pageant at Windsor

My mother was a member of the Cookham Dean WI. There was only one group in those days for all three villages, and they would meet at the old Drill Hall where the village hall now stands. In 1928 we took part in an historical pageant in the Windsor Home Park. I remember the music and horses very clearly. Each WI represented a different reign, and Cookham Dean represented George I and 'Agriculture'. We took the sign from the 'Hare and Hounds' with us, I can't remember why.

Frances Harvey, born 1918.

Joining the WI

The first thing I joined was the Afternoon WI I was one of the founding members with Mrs Hayward Browne, who was the first President. I was not a very good member because they met in the afternoon and I always had things to do. It was much better when we started an evening group in 1953 with Mrs Saunders and Mrs Andrews. I really became involved then. I was the first President, knowing nothing about what I should be doing! I don't think the meetings have changed much. We had a speaker, dances, dramas all sorts of things.

Vivien Jerome (Mrs Ripley), born 1909.

Fun with the Horticultural Society

I first got involved with the Horticultural Society in the 1960s. We would always have over a hundred people come to Pinder Hall. There was a good mix of people – Mrs

The W.I. pageant rehearsal in 1928.

Manners Wood and Colonel Vanderfelt would come, and all the local people too. Mr Ridgley ran the meetings and was so prim and proper, always a nice navy blue suit, white shirt and immaculate polished black shoes. I can see him now with his rosy cheeks. It was ever so friendly. Husband and wife would come together. Ken Tuck used to stand by the door and greet everyone as they came in. We would have a speaker, or occasionally a film or slides, or practical advice. We would have a big raffle, and everybody would bring something. The table would be covered. People would bring in a packet of tea, or a bag of sugar and stuff like that. Mr Ridgley always had surprises for us. He would have what he called his 'behind the curtain' prizes, and they'd be things like a nice pot plant or a big potato!. Everybody did things and they did it freely. We would have a big dinner and that was very dressed-up. We would have it in Pinder Hall. The Horticultural Club had three shows a year, one in early June for the Sweet Peas, then late July or August, and then the late show for Chrysanthemums and things. They would be in various places, Dean Meadow, Pinder Hall, Church Hall, all around the place. We had BBC *Gardeners' Question Time* in Pinder Hall once in the sixties. Fred Loades and Bill Sowerbutts were on the panel. The committee did the catering, and we did a country meal and we got a letter from the BBC saying how good it was. Everything was fresh cooked. Doug Godfrey was chairman then, and he was a butcher. We had an ox tongue, which I cooked, and he salted a leg of pork so we had boiled salt pork. We had a wonderful team that was pleased to do it.

Mabel Vevers.

Competitive gardeners

Father was a cottage gardener. He didn't do gardening for a living, so he wasn't in the same class as the great gardeners like Mr Lewington and Mr Tomlin. My father was an excellent gardener. Every August Monday was the Cookham Dean show in Mrs Rowe's Dean Croft, which stretched all the way down to the back of the Chequers. Father's competition came from Mr Maine who was a bricklayer by trade and lived down the bottom of Bigfrith and Mr King, who lived up at Tugwood, who was also a bricklayer's labourer and a jobbing gardener. They won for years on end. They used to go to Summerleaze Show and the big one was Cox Green. Father's allotment was where the school house is now, and when they got turfed off there he went up to Mount Hill up by Spring Lane.

John Taft, born 1922.

Cookham highlights

The highlights of the year in Cookham were the regattas in the summer and the flower shows. They used to alternate between Moor Hall and Lullebrook Manor. My father used to do the catering for them both. The regatta was in Bell Rope Meadow. It was quite a big affair and we would have rowing eights from all over the place. There was also a huge fair on the moor for each occasion. They were real village things, but they did attract a lot of people.

Kate Swan, born 1911.

Collecting wasp nests

My dad told me once about the fête they used to have on the Cricket Common in Cookham Dean. There used to be a competition to see who could collect the most wasp nests and one year he won it with 180 nests! He got them from all over

Cookham Dean – with all the fruit around. It was about the only work they could get that year, the farmers would pay them to take them away.

Leslie Knight, born 1923.

The bell-ringers

My sister lived in Cookham – she was married to the local dairyman Ernie Tuck. Both my sister and her husband were bell-ringers – so I rang the bells on my first visit to Cookham. I've been involved with the Church ever since. All the pews behind the font were reserved for the bell-ringers, there could be about thirty people waiting to ring in those days (1930s) and it was always packed on Tuesdays the practice night. It was a good chance to get together.

Eddie Smyth, born 1909.

Finding ammunition

As a teenager in the fifties we had a lot more freedom because there wasn't the danger there is now. When they cut the grass down we made camps and we used to enjoy sliding down the railway arch in Terrys Lane. The arch down there was like sheer glass, it was wonderful. We used to go up to the railway bridge, sit on the top and slide down the arch. There was an ammunition dump by the side of the railway and we used to go down there and pick all the bullets out.

Jeanette Roll (Edwards), born 1941.

The Kaffirs of Cookham Dean

The village green (the Cricket Common) was the central meeting place for people. We had the Drill Hall where we would have whist drives and dances and it was used as a

Holy Trinity bellringers.

Kaffir's New Years Eve party, 1925.

youth club. There was a snooker table and we'd play table tennis. There used to be lots of concerts. The Kaffirs had a concert party who would put on shows. My father and my uncle did lots of sketches. My Uncle Fred was nicknamed 'Whacker' and my Dad was called 'Paddy'. Ted Skegg would do a bit of singing and we had Horace Spencer, Stanley's brother, who would do card shows.

Pat Woodbridge, born 1927.

Happy times

We used to have a choir and at Christmas we would go carol singing. We were invited to Dial Close and Frosts in Church Road to sing at their dinner parties. Then we would have mince pies and I have very happy memories of the carol singing. The moon always seemed to shine on those occasions. I had a wonderful childhood.

Kate Swan, born 1911.

Drinks at six

Before the war my mother, Marjorie Castellanos, used to entertain a lot in the house. A very favoured pastime was to have drinks at six o'clock. At other times there would be people coming to dinner and they all wore evening dress. As a child I was sometimes brought down to meet them. I always admired their dresses and jewellery, but my earliest memory of Cookham is being taken for walks all the time. The walks seemed immensely long. In those days we were very heavily dressed. I remember I had sort of two-piece suit made out of Harris Tweed with gaiters of Harris Tweed and a little coat.

Esilda Mezulianik, born 1929.

The pigmaphone

Sometimes on my afternoon off I would go to the cinema in Bourne End with a friend, or stay at home and play cards or Ludo. We had a little 'pigmaphone' at Albion Cottages in Cookham Dean. It was square with a trumpet on it like a small gramophone that we played records on. We thought that was wonderful. We had 'The Laughing Policeman' and just a couple of others.

Nancy Harvey, born 1916.

The Cookham Cossacks

The Cookham Cossacks were great. They were a group of lads who ran a cycle speedway team. It was push-bikes – pedal power. They had awful trouble at first finding somewhere to race, and in the end they had it by the Black Bridge on the golf course, on the river side. It was just a round circuit. They were great – they won all sorts of things. They were between about sixteen and thirty, and couldn't do it for very long because of National Service. We were in a league and when we had to travel they all used to put their bikes on Jim East's coal cart, and his father would come and drive a huge big car. It

was like a circus leaving town. There'd be a dozen bikes at least.

Margaret Tuck, born 1937.

Sunday best

Sundays in Cookham Dean were a day for Sunday best clothes that you didn't wear in the week. I used to go to church at eleven o'clock and then again for Sunday school at three o'clock, which was run by Kathy Ricketts. Sunday evening was a family time. We used to go off for a walk, sometimes down through the fields to Cockmarsh to the old pub called The Quarry down by the river, sometimes we used to walk through Quarry Woods and down across the fields to The Bull at Bisham, and then other times we might just do a walk round the village and that took a long time because everyone you passed you spoke to – everyone knew everybody, they were all born here and their families grew up here.

Gordon Harris, born 1932.

A Jubilee Procession on 6 May 1935.

The Lord's day

Grandma was a strict Victorian Methodist. On Sunday we went to the Methodist chapel in Cookham Rise four times a day. There was no radio, no washing, no nothing – it was the Lord's day and that was it. You only sat and read or did knitting, you didn't go out except to church.

Jeanette Roll (Edwards), born 1941.

Servants to church

I always used to go to Sunday school at Holy Trinity in the afternoon. The vicar, Hayward Browne, would take it. Then we would go to Evensong. Most of the village went to church then. You were brought up to go. Most of the people round here had been in service before they were married, and so you automatically went to church. If you were in service you had to go with your employer.

Nancy James, born 1927.

Make our own entertainment

We had to make our own entertainment. The boys played cricket and boys and girls together in teams used to play 'tracking' and lay trails for each other. There wasn't much other entertainment, it was wartime and there was the blackout so you didn't reckon to go out at night. You made your own entertainment at home, listening to the radio and sitting and talking to each other in the evenings.

Gordon Harris, born 1932.

Royal celebrations

There was a big procession for George V's Jubilee in 1935. I'd never seen one before and if I remember it right it came up from Cookham to Jordan's Field, which is at the side of Dean Lane. The football club and the cricket clubs were in it and Hardings the builders had a lorry full of their employees all decorated. All three of the Cookhams got

The Silver Jubilee Pageant, 1935.

together to celebrate, which was quite unusual. We had commemorative mugs and spoons.

Pat Woodbridge, born 1927.

All hands to the pump

I remember very well in Jordon's field (Dean Meadow) there was an enormous celebration for the 1936 coronation. There were various pet shows and we entered our bulldog Bill, who got into a fight with a goat! The Fire Brigade were due to take part in a display with their new engine. They had built a house out of wood which was set alight. The hose pipes were turned on and nothing happened – it was eventually discovered that Captain Phillips (the honorary head if the Fire Brigade) had parked his brand new grey Chrysler on top of the hose! By the time the hose was working there wasn't a trace of house left, just a mass of smouldering embers.

Esilda Mezulianik, born 1929.

The May Queen's attendant

All I can remember of King George's VI Coronation – we were from the three schools – Gwen Tisdale was from Cookham Rise school, she was the May Queen. I was sitting at her feet, and there were four of us from Holy Trinity and four from Cookham Dean. The horse and cart came from Lord Astor's farm, and we went from the Village up to Dean Lane. We had sports and there was a fair. There were lots of floats in the parade. There was a cattle show. It was fine day.

Nancy James, born 1927.

Nancy James at the May Queen's feet, 1936.

Celebrating the Queen's Silver Jubilee in 1977.

Bitterly cold

The main thing I remember about the Queen's Coronation in 1953 was that it was bitterly cold. We had a celebration in the field at Dean Lane in Cookham Rise. It was like a winter's day and Aunt Daisy took us back to her house and boiled us all an egg for tea and made us a nice hot cup of tea at her house in Grange Road.

Nancy Harvey, born 1918.

Pouring with rain

We had a tent for the 1953 Coronation and I sang duets with somebody. People from the village came to watch. It was a terribly wet day so they gradually moved away and in the end Stanley Spencer was the only one left sitting there! I've never forgotten that.

Sonia Redway, born 192°7.

Early television

We had a television. It was a lovely old Baird, with a reflecting screen. It was a solid wooden case the size of a table with a lift up lid with a big mirror on it. You watched the reflection of the picture on the screen in the mirror. People came from all over the district to see it, and on Coronation Day we all squashed into our room. My husband opened some champagne and we were still there at eleven o'clock at night watching the fireworks.

Mabel Vevers.

Street party

We had a street party for the Silver Jubilee. There were hundreds of people. I remember doing sandwiches in the International – the shop was closed, so we used the space. Twelve of us made hundreds and hundreds of sandwiches. I can still see my mother hanging out of the bedroom window watching. It was a very cold wet day. They used our house for water when they painted the Union Jack on the street. They had a platform by the War Memorial where they had dancing, and a big bonfire on the moor in the evening.

Nancy James, born 1927.

9 Wartime

The beginning of the war

I was twelve when war broke out, in fact I remember it starting. I had just gone down to the secondary school when school was abandoned for a while. We were off for about three or four weeks. We used to go out and play. There were lots of evacuees, and it was difficult trying to get used to their ways. We called each teacher 'Miss', they called him or her 'Mam' and because a lot of them came from the East End they had Cockney slang. There was never any friction and we got on quite well with them. We stayed in touch with some of them for years after the war. I remember the first night they came round with the gas masks, it frightened me. We had the blackout with the curtains and everything. Most of the older children, like Brian and Henry Taft, had to go to fight. Henry was killed. During the war there was tremendous comradeship, everybody came together and I think this is what happened with the evacuees. We all worked together.

Pat Woodbridge, born 1927.

The fire brigade

I joined the local fire brigade as a part-timer during the war. Cookham was a full-time station with sixty firemen in those days. They

Remembrance Day Dinner, Athletic Hall, 1921.

were based in the Athletic Hall in Berries road and had two fire engines and two trainer pumps. We were on general call out and could be called out to Portsmouth and Southampton when they were being bombed. A crew of seven men would take a fire engine and sometimes stay down there for a week at a time as standbys. Our brigade went up when the Queens Hall in London was on fire. Our fire engine had old fashioned solid tyres and of course when we got to London with all the broken glass they said 'Eh, we're keeping that', and they sent us home with a brand new fire engine!

Eddie Smyth, born 1909.

Problems with evacuees

We had three evacuees in the house, two grown ups and a young boy called Malcolm. Mrs Glindon was one of them, but I can't remember the other lady's name at all. They didn't come through the billeting officer, because the evacuees that were supposed to come to Cookham went to the wrong place. They went to Crookham in Hampshire instead. My father was gardener at John Lewis's, so we had people from there. It was difficult to fit them all in the house. The little boy was only four and he slept in the same bedroom as my parents. I slept in the front room with the old lady and the other young lady had the back bedroom, because we only had two bedrooms and two rooms downstairs. Malcolm was awful. He wouldn't eat and my poor mother would cry trying to get him to eat. Unfortunately he got friendly with some children who lived at the end of the road and they were all playing out in the fields, and he got some matches off of my mother's cooker. They'd set fire to a hayrick out in Marsh Meadows. My mother was very upset about it, and made his parents take him back! The older lady stayed with us

Eddie Smyth in his fireman's uniform, 1940.

most of the war, but the younger one didn't stay very long. They all used to come at the weekends, the little boy's parents would come out, and the older lady's husband from Lambeth. Mother had to feed them all, and none of them ever brought food with them. We had their ration books, and my father got extra cheese because he was classed as an agricultural worker. I remember going to Burgesses with our sugar rations, we had two ounces of butter and a little sugar, and they would let us have some chocolate without sweet coupons. I don't know if that was legal!

Nancy James, born 1927.

Leaving London

We came to Cookham, to the Odney Club, the week before war was declared in 1939. My husband worked for John Lewis and it was very good of Speden Lewis to put out the offer for wives and children to come to Cookham – in the event of there being a war, they could apply. I didn't want to come to Cookham, I didn't want to come out of London and then I never wanted to go back afterwards. We were attached to the Odney Club, we had all of the amenities and we had the grounds and we were catered for. Speden Lewis was a lovely humane man; he was a disciplinarian but he was fair. We were one of the only families who stayed in Cookham. Nearly all the others went back because no bombs dropped at the beginning of the war and they missed London. The housekeeper, Mrs Reed at Odney thought she ought to do something because there were so many children and so she organized a pantomime. My daughter Nina was a fairy and my son Godfrey was a pixie. After we had been there a while, the Price Davies who were running the Odney Club asked if we could give a hand because all of the waitresses had been taken for war jobs. Later on there were American soldiers at Odney. I thought they rather mucked the club up, they were a bit boisterous and know-it-all.

Rene Allen, born 1906.

Evacuees were friends

When the evacuees came to Cookham Dean school they brought their own headmaster,

The evacuees panto at Odney, Christmas 1939. Nina Allen is the fairy at the top and Godfrey is in the middle of the front row.

Mr Matthews, and another teacher called Miss Wootten. At the end of the year they got married! The evacuees were taught at the school – they had tried to keep the two lots separate at the start but it didn't work so we all just mixed in together. In the end we got on very well together. We had one or two little problems on the first day or two; the evacuees were at one end of the school yard and we were at the other and we thought what's going to happen here? But at the end of the day I had some good friends in the evacuees.

Gordon Harris, born 1932.

Housekeeper unhappy

We had a couple of evacuees staying with us at Rowborough. Head, the housekeeper, put her foot down to try and put it off as much as possible. The first ones that were due to come were in the group that got sent to Crookham by mistake, but we had to have some from the next lot. We had two mothers with their children. The dining room was turned in to their eating and sitting room, and they had rooms upstairs, but Head would not let them have the kitchen. She had to feed them, and they didn't like her food, so that didn't work very well. They also wanted their husbands down, and Head didn't like that either, so they all decided the bombs were better and cleared off back to London.

Vivien Jerome (Mrs Ripley) born 1909.

Mucked in

The evacuees at school came from Hackney I think. They came up to Cookham Dean school which was crowded and were billeted in the big houses around. We all mucked in together. There's a family of brothers that I left school with, worked with in different

places, went to Army and Sea Cadets with and I still see now, who were evacuees. Some stayed here after the war and their mums and dads came down and got council houses. It changed their lives.

Ray Nash, born 1929.

Crowding didn't mean a thing

During the height of the bombing during the 1940 Battle of Britain, scores of people were just coming out of London with anything they could get hold of. There were three very big furniture lorries going along Whyteladyes Lane. They were knocking on doors – 'Could you take a family in?' My mother took in two. We used to call them Uncle Wal and Rose. They had been bombed out. The husband was in the fire service so he had to go back, and the woman was in a terrible state. The first night that she was there I remember the sirens going and of course to us it didn't mean a lot because we didn't see anything much. She was really frightened and it took her a long time to get used to it and realize she was safe. Of course crowding didn't mean a thing in those days. There would be about ten of us and only three bedrooms. You slept on the floor and did the best you could. At the height of it the Drill Hall in Cookham Dean was used as a stop-gap for putting people up. We would listen to the radio in the evenings as the only form of entertainment. At school we had two German refugees – Gerhardt Slazenger who spoke really good English and another boy who could hardly speak a word, and through that I think I took an interest in the war. Gerhardt would tell us about what was happening in Germany and how he got out. They created quite a lot of interest, there was no prejudice. People didn't know what was going on at the time.

Pat Woodbridge, born 1927.

Resentment

During the war there were two gangs: them (the evacuees) and us. We slightly resented the evacuees because we thought they had all these special privileges as people were trying to be nice to them since they were away from home. We didn't get anything like that so there was always an armed truce.

Keith Hatch and Barry Hatch,
born 1932 and 1935.

Jealousy

My son was brought up by his gran. She used to look after him, she always had him at weekends, and then it got to be that he stayed there in the week and then never came back. She lived in Apsley Cottages on Lower Road. He did come back once during the war, when she took in an evacuee. Ray didn't like him, so he came back home. He soon went back to her though.

Connie Fenner, born 1910.

The lookout

I was the aircraft spotter for Cookham Rise school. I was keen on aeroplanes and could tell which one was which. When the air-raid siren went off Mr Wood used to send me off into the playground looking for German planes. If I saw any planes, then I would have to go in and tell them, and then everyone would have to get under their desks! I don't ever remember seeing any German planes though.

John Tubb, born 1928.

The Home Guard

During the Second World War because my father was a baker, which was a reserved occupation, he was in the local Home Guard. I remember him in his Home Guard uniform with a rifle and a bayonet. He got a nasty cut on the leg from an accident with the bayonet. At the bottom of Quarry Woods opposite what is now Longridge

The Cookham Dean Home Guard Platoon, 1941.

Scout Camp was the Home Guard rifle range. The remains of the targets are still there. They used .303 Lee Enfield rifles. As boys we were very interested in the war; it was a great adventure for us.

Tony Deadman, born 1936.

One rifle between them

There was a retired bank manager called Mr Crowe who lived in Badgers; he used to man the lookout post for the Home Guard in Cookham Dean. It was up on Standing, up towards the woods opposite the National Trust car park. They had an old shepherd's hut in the wood up there, and he had the rifle. There was only one rifle between them, and I don't think they had any ammunition. When the air raid sounded he used to run up there to man the post, but nine times out of ten when he got there the siren had stopped, and the all-clear was sounded. My dad was in the Home Guard and we used to have a laugh about it. They used to man this post all night long and my mum used to get fed up with it. They'd hold manoeuvres on Sunday morning, and invariably end up in the Jolly Farmer. They'd have bags of chalk as make-believe bombs to throw at each other.

Jack Tomlin, born 1927.

Cookham Home Guard

I was in the Home Guard, like Private Pike, the youngest, trying to keep up with everything. My duty was to carry the Browning Automatic Rifle, the heaviest thing we had to carry. We had a hut at the Crown, where we would parade. We did most of our patrols on Sunday morning, because everyone was working. Our actual duty was protecting Cookham Bridge, and we had a nightly patrol. We had a little hut by the bridge, and would take it in turns to stand guard. This one Sunday morning we were having an exercise, attacking Cookham Bridge. Half of us were defending, and half attacking. We came in to Cookham through School Lane, and there were about three of us that went over the garden fence, when round the corner came a bull terrier. We retreated very quickly.

John Field, born 1924.

Prisoners help on the farm

Cookham Dean Common was cleared by Italian prisoners during the war and was all corn during the last years of the war. We had some Germans from a local camp who came to help us on the farm with the growing of the vegetables.

Ralph Thompson, born 1913.

Italians paint the bridge

I remember seeing the Italian POWs up Terrys Lane. They had a hut up there and they had built a bonfire. They were making toast by it and I felt very sorry for them. They were there because they were painting the railway bridge.

Margaret Tuck, born 1937.

On the river

My Aunt Biddy (my dad's sister) took over running the ferry during the First World War while my grandfather went in the services. During the Second World War I was working as a boat builder and we came under the Admiralty. I couldn't leave Woottens and they couldn't sack me. We built little dinghies for MTB tenders, for going ashore from big boats. Then we built twenty foot

Aunt Biddy manning the ferry in 1918.

long cutters which went out to the Far East, for taking crews from ship to shore.

John Brooks, born 1923.

Women go to work

I was working in Bourne End during the war. I did four and a half years at the aircraft factory which was at Andrews Boathouses. One was turned into a tool shop and we made the ribs which went inside the wings of spitfires. I worked in dispatch – they called it my rabbit hutch. One week when the floods came up we had to have a week off. We shouldn't have been pleased but we were!

Nancy Harvey, born 1916.

The Kings Arms factory

I worked at the factory that opened at the

back of The Kings Arms, making parts for aeroplanes. We had to wind copper wire around a piece of metal. The lady in charge was called Mrs Mowbray-Greene and she was well up in society; there were a lot of us working in there, it was quite a big room .

Rene Allen, born 1906.

Making do

I left school during the war and trained as a couture dressmaker in Cookham High Street. We used to work from garages at the back of a little shop near the Kings Arms. During the war we made ladies suits out of men's evening suits. They were all away in the forces and the wives would bring in their dress suits and have them made into suits for themselves. We used to un-pick them and a pair of trousers would make a straight skirt and a jacket could be made into a ladies jacket. We used to reverse and turn them. My father did ARP – Air Raid Patrol. He used to go out on patrol at night, and made us do the blackout. We had wooden boards that fitted in to the windows. We had a great big cement block outside the house that was supposed to be a road block for if there was an invasion. They had a tree trunk on the other side of the road that they were supposed to wheel across. So a log was Cookham's defence against the German invasion! We had sand bags on the pavement, because I remember sitting on them to play.

Nancy James, born 1927.

Part-time firewoman

I was a part-time firewoman during the war in the Village. My duties were to go down and sit in the fire station (Berries road) and mark in the book when the men came on duty, and to take any fire calls. I went to work for the

Air Transport Auxiliary, which was based at White Waltham Airfield. I did the salaries of all the flying staff, there were several thousand of them. They came from America, Canada, France, Chile, many countries. Every plane that was in the air during the war was flown from the factory to the aerodromes by the ATA, who recruited pilots who were too old or unfit to be in the RAF. The girls did sometimes upset me in my department. A lot of them had never worked before and came from well-to-do families who got them in to the ATA to avoid them being called up. They'd get in late in the morning and sit on their desks smoking. A lot of them had husbands on the front line. These girls went out every night with the American and Canadian pilots.

Frances Harvey, born 1918.

Firewoman Frances Harvey during the war.

Bombs drop

One frightening thing I remember in Cookham was one Sunday morning about ten o'clock there was this tremendous drone of a plane diving very low – you just assumed it was one of ours. All of a sudden 'boom boom boom' it dropped about seven fifty-pounders along Whyteladyes. One dropped in a garden and one dropped in where the cricket pitch now is. One went further over but it was scary.

Pat Woodbridge, born 1927.

Taking shelter

One or two bombs were dropped – the Germans were getting rid of them before they went home. One night mum and I were out walking and a plane came over and we ducked down behind the barn and he dropped his bombs down on Widbrook, I think. You could hear the bombs being dropped, and Mum and I crouched down under the barn.

Lucy Edwards, born 1914.

Too embarrassed

Doreen and I were walking up Dean Lane when a doodle bug came over. We were walking up with our bikes and we were too embarrassed to lie on the floor when the engine cut out! Typical English, we couldn't lie down and get our clothes all dirty! It's daft when you think about it. It went off down in Marlow somewhere.

John Tubb, born 1928.

Fun and games

We had a great time during the war. We had

everybody down here – the Americans, the Polish pilots and all sorts. We had more men here than we'd ever seen. We had dances at the Pinder Hall. The Americans took over Odney, and you couldn't go down the lane. I was riding down there one night on my bike and I heard 'Halt – who goes there?' and I thought 'What on earth was that?'. He went 'Stop' and he shone his light and there was this big American with his tin hat. I went 'Who are you?' and he said 'More to the point Madam who are you?' I said I was Doreen Harris and I was going on down the road. He said 'Oh no you're not – I want to see your identity card' 'My identity card,' I said, 'I don't carry that because my mum says I'll lose it!' It only had a number on and your name,

no photograph or anything. I got to know dozens of Americans, and we had a really nice time. It was great. Bomber Command was based up in Cookham Dean at the Hockett and there were Polish pilots up there who would click their heels and were so polite. The Polish pilots would go into the Jolly Farmer and they were so nice. The British Army were up at the Brick Kiln.

Doreen Tubb (Harris), born 1926.

Soldiers billet

I was ten at the beginning of the war – it was a big joke to us at ten years old, the troops came round here and took over the brick

Brick Kiln Billet.

kiln. The big kiln and the drying sheds were billets and the soldiers had to live in there. There were the Manchester and Devonshire Regiments. The Home Guard had a lookout at the top of Shepherds Standing and they were watching for parachutists that never came. We had four bombs up at the Mount which killed four horses, and we had nine down Cookham. We watched a most marvellous dogfight, Spitfires or Hurricanes, we were just coming out of school – a big raid of German bombers going over. The Germans released their bombs here, they went in a path from Bisham church up the river, two or three of them went in the river and right across the top of Oxford Road to the waterworks. There was one man killed there. The river was alive with fish where they'd blown them up there. As boys if ever we heard anything going on – we were there. Down the bottom at Furze Platt there were landmines at Mr Pursers Farm at Cannon Court.

Ray Nash, born 1929.

Under the table

My dad went in the navy, and we didn't see him for about four years. We used to sleep underneath the table, especially when Coventry was on. We saw the Blitz in London – the red glow in the sky. When they raided Coventry they came over here. Oh the drone, you'd never heard anything like it, it was dreadful. Wave after wave of planes came over. We guessed what had happened, although we didn't know where they were going. They'd told us to sleep by a wall, so we were under the table downstairs, pushed up against the wall. That was just that one night.

Ray Fenner, born 1935.

Girls' Training Corps

I organized the Girls' Training Corps during the war. Mr Pinder Brown decided that we needed one in Cookham and asked me to organize it. I said I didn't know anything about it and he said that didn't matter. He said his daughter Gwen Pinder-Brown would help. We only had about ten girls, and they would stand to attention, and I would go and inspect their ranks, and we never really knew what the point of it was, or what we were supposed to do! I remember Doreen Tubb, and Jean Gigg was a very good member. We had lots of good ideas, like going on map reading exercises. I'm not sure we ever did it though! I do remember they didn't use deodorant at that time, and having to tell the girls that they ought to use it. I got terribly tied up trying to tell the girls that they were smelling rather... it was like trying to tell them about sex for the first time! It was fairly chaotic and Gwen was getting fed up with it. We decided to disband, but I remember Mr Pinder-Brown being very upset that we had decided to give up.

Vivien Jerome (Mrs Ripley), born 1909.

War work for girls

We had a Girls' Training Corps. What they trained us for I don't know, but we wore a forage cap and a navy blue skirt, white blouse and a navy blue jumper. We used to go to Pinder Hall and march around. Miss Pinder-Brown and Mrs Ripley were our officers, and they said 'Would you like to do some war work? and we said 'Yes we'd love to do that'. So they took us up to Harwood and we would cut out patterns for pyjamas for war-wounded in hospital. I can see these patterns now, and the maid would bring us in beautiful long glasses of lemonade.

Doreen Tubb (Harris), 1926.

GTC sergeant

During the war we joined the Girls' Training Corps and had great fun. We held meetings at Pinder Hall. I became a sergeant and enjoyed drilling. We also did keep fit at Herries school.

Jean Gigg (Hobbs) born 1926.

Gas masks

I remember having a gas mask which we had to take to school with us. We used to have to test them with a piece of blotting paper. You'd put on your mask and suck through it and try to get the blotting paper to stick to it. If there was an air raid we'd go under the stairs, but there really wasn't much activity.

Margaret Tuck, born 1937.

The land girls

I was the Welfare Officer for the Land Army girls. I had about ten girls, and I had to go along and see them and check out that they were alright. They came from all over the country. Farmer Parsons really objected when I came and chatted to the girls. He didn't like me taking them away from their work. He lived in Poundfield and farmed round there. We spread them around the area, but I don't remember there being many of them at all. I'd always wanted to keep bees and when the war came you could get extra sugar for them. If you had bees and had an out apiary you could get extra petrol coupons to visit your bees. The high-ups never realised you didn't visit them in the winter – so I had petrol to get around with. During the war I would do the Christmas post round in the pony and trap. In those days you would get a post on Christmas Day. They always asked for volunteers a couple of weeks before Christmas to deliver it, so I did it with the pony and trap. I would take the postman with me, and we would go round and empty the pillar boxes and Mrs Bromley would always give the pony a bun when we passed. So of course the pony learnt that every time he saw a pillar box or passed the bakery he should stop!

Vivien Jerome (Mrs Ripley), born 1909.

Practice on the baby

When I was in the Girl Guides we had that in the Kings Hall (The Spencer Gallery). We had to learn first aid and during the war we would practise with stirrup pumps. We had to practise running messages, morse-code and

Jean Hobbs (later Gigg), Sergeant in the GTC.

Nancy James in the Girl Guides.

semaphore. I was also a Sea Ranger and we would do ARP drill. The vicar of All Saints let us practise putting his baby in the baby gas mask. In the Guides we did a lot of fundraising for the War Effort. We would have raffles and sales that we would make things for.

Nancy James, born 1927.

Rations

They were hard times, but we were happy! Everyone pulled together. I was twenty-one when war broke out. It was wonderful. The rations of course were very strict. I had an ulcer so I had a little slip that I could take to the War Office. The ration of milk was a third of a pint a day, there were no eggs only egg powder, but because of my illness I was allowed a pint of milk a day and one fresh egg a week.

Frances Harvey, born 1918.

School dinners

At dinnertime we used to walk down from Cookham Dean school – march down in a blooming great big crocodile down to the Young Mens Club (where the Village Hall is now) and the dinners were cooked there by two ladies, Emily and Mrs Evans. We had great dinners, nearly always stew and a dumpling, but it was a meal – don't forget food wasn't always plentiful in wartime. Nearly every day for sweet we had semolina with jam in it.

Gordon Harris, born 1932.

Treats

At the end of the war we had ice creams again. There were no wafers, just ice cream in blocks wrapped up in paper, 3d bars. Cookham Dean school would finish at five to twelve one week, and Holy Trinity at five to twelve the next, so we could all belt to the sweet shop in Cookham Rise to get our ice creams. One Sunday we all biked from here to Whipsnade Zoo because we knew we could get ice creams! You didn't think anything of going long distances on a bike in those days.

Ray Fenner, born 1935.

Wartime wedding

I met my husband during the war at the Ferry Hotel. I had gone there to look after the children of the landlords, Mr and Mrs Thursby. I then started to work behind the bar. I didn't get called up because all the troops came round here, and they needed bar staff. My husband was stationed at the Odney Club. He came from Chichester and was in the Royal Sussex Regiment. He had been through Dunkirk before he came, and he hadn't had a very easy time. He didn't tell me much about it. Percy was away off and on throughout the war. We did our courting by post. I knew him six years before we married, and I doubt I saw him for more than six weeks. We got married in 1945 in Cookham church. My grandmother was amazing – how she got all the stuff together I'll never know. She made my wedding cake – a two-tier cake, and of course his leave kept being put off. You couldn't get marzipan icing then, you just had some kind of yellow paste to put under the icing. The trouble was the colour would come through the white icing if you left it on too long. Grandmother used to look at it and say, 'are you sure he's coming, because if not, soon you'll have yellow icing on the cake!' I had my banns ready, we were supposed to get married in January and we ended up getting married in June. It was a gorgeous sunny day. My grandmother had a big reception for us in Ross Cottage and she'd made everything, all the food. The vicar was Hayward Browne. We went down to see him the night before the wedding and he had a swing hammock in the garden. We sat in there and I remember him saying 'I hope you'll be very happy' – and we were.

Joan Stringer, born 1922.

Joan and Percy Stringer married at Holy Trinity church.

Home-made trousseau

We got married in 1948. Clothing was still on coupons, so all the family had to save their coupons so that I could have a white wedding and I had three bridesmaids which took rather a lot of coupons. I made my own trousseau. They advertised in the paper parachutes for sale so I sent away for a parachute and I managed to make all sorts of things; nightdresses, cami-knickers and slips. I sent

Jean and Peter Gigg at Cookham Dean church in 1948.

away for another parachute but it was a much stiffer material, so I stuck to the first one.

Jean Gigg (Hobbs), born 1926.

Moor Hall

I left school in 1941 and went to Moor Hall to live and work. Odeon Cinemas owned it and moved all their offices out of London to Cookham and I stayed there all through the war working in the accounts department. Dances were a regular thing there and they used to put on some shows, but mostly normal entertainment like singers and comedians. Freda Salberg was the house-keeper and organised all sorts of things. Immediately after the war J. Arthur Rank set up Gaumont British Animations and what he wanted to do was to set up a rival for Walt Disney making animated pictures. One of the animators I remember was Bob Monkhouse.

They didn't mention that on *This is Your Life!*

Pat Woodbridge, born 1927.

Pulling together

Freda 'Sally' Salberg could fix anything. She knew people in London in the theatrical, radio and film world. Every time we had a big savings drive she would arrange for a dance at Moor Hall, and she would get people like Henry Hall and his Orchestra, Vic Oliver, Bebe Daniels, and Ben Lyon. Chesney and Allen to come down. Everybody wanted to get tickets to get in. The war made the whole village pull together. To raise money we had 'War Weapons Week', 'Wings for Victory', 'Warships Week', saving stamps and we had dances. There were whist drives nearly every other night of the week. The working men's club had one, the Women's Institute had one. They held theirs at the Women's Institute Hall at the top of Kennel Lane. It was a tin clad hut, with lovely wooden paneling inside. I remember coming down Kennel Lane during the Blitz and looking over towards Cliveden, and you could see the anti-aircraft fire just like a firework display all over the sky. The class structure of the Village began to break down during the war. We pulled together as a team.

James Hatch, born 1930.

Good spirit

I think the war years meant quite a lot to everybody. We were all working together – the farm workers just accepted me as one of them. There was a good spirit in the war and during the years afterwards even though we were very short of everything and life was tough. In the arts everything came to life – it was great.

Ralph Thompson, born 1913.

VE Day

During the war we were living in a caravan at Strande Castle. We used to meet friends on a Saturday morning for coffee and cakes at the Copper Kettle. In spite of rationing the cakes were memorable. During the final blast of the Blitz tents appeared in the field by us and people came from London to sleep overnight. Eventually VE day arrived and we celebrated with the village on Cookham Moor with dancing and a bonfire.

Joan Holt, born 1920.

Father returns

When I came back from Burma in November 1945 I felt very cold. It was a job trying to acclimatise yourself, adjust yourself. You came back into civvy street – you've got no real home of your own, just living with your in-laws so you'd got to bide your tongue. You've got no home, you've got no money and you've got no job. You've got to try and adjust, and you've got a child (aged six) who looks on you as a complete stranger who'd come in and tried to take her grandad's place, because she'd always looked on her grandad as her father. That was the difficulty of us servicemen – coming back to adjust to these positions.

Sydney Edwards, born 1918.

The daughter

It was hard for me when my dad come home from the war – I didn't know who he was. My first memory I have of dad he came into the bedroom and he had this khaki outfit on with this bush hat… it terrified the life out of me.

Jeanette Roll (Edwards) born 1941.

The mother

Although I brought her up with his photograph, he was still a stranger. I was piggy in the middle – with him and her and my mum and dad, who we lived with. Syd wouldn't talk and I wouldn't ask what he'd been through and mum wanted him to tell us and Jeanette was awkward. Lots of families went through the same.

Lucy Edwards, born 1914.

Left behind

When the Americans left Cookham they left a dog behind. He followed my son Michael home once, and decided to stay with us. I feel sure he had belonged to a soldier who couldn't take him with him when he left, because he would go charging up to any soldier that he saw. So he stayed with us and we kept him until he was about seventeen. He was called 'Billy' and was very well known in Cookham in those days. He was very polite and a very good guard dog. There wasn't a window he couldn't open. We would perhaps go down to the pub for a drink, and leave him shut up in the house. Suddenly he would appear beside you in the pub, having broken out of the house.

Vivien Jerome (Mrs Ripley), born 1909.

10 Stanley Spencer

Growing up with Stanley Spencer

I was born on Stanley Spencer's twentieth birthday and I grew up with him, knowing he was a painter with Gilbert (his brother), and my brother and I used to follow them around and watch them painting; that would have been in the early twenties. I well remember going and sitting beside him whilst he painted that picture of the May Tree in Marsh Meadows. You learnt not to speak to him when he was painting because he was so engrossed in what he was doing. Stanley's

Sir Stanley Spencer compares hands with the Ferryman in 1958. (Photograph by Eileen and Leslie Gibbon.)

father gave me my first music lessons, so I used to go over to the house (Fernlea). There was a grand piano in the drawing room, which we played on, and there was a lovely Spanish shawl thrown over the top with a lot of family pictures on the top of it. There was also an upright piano in the dining room.

Kate Swan, born 1911.

First meeting

My parents had moved to Cookham and because I had been at art college I had seen an Arts Council film about Stanley Spencer. The very day that the removal van was outside our house a man came walking down the street, in a long black coat and he had white hair and glasses and I said 'Are you

The Spencer family outside Fernlea in the High Street.

Stanley Spencer?' and he said 'Yes I am' so I said 'Well, I'm an artist too!' and he was very happy about that and laughed and twinkled. He told me to come and see him any time I wanted to. I was nearly nineteen years old. I couldn't wait to get up there and see him. When I saw his bedroom it was incredible – it was just full of this brilliant painting 'The Crucifixion'. He showed me some sketches. They were often tiny, you wouldn't believe anybody could work from such tiny sketches, on the back of envelopes etc. He showed me things from before that and things that were on the way and things that were ideas for the future. He told me he used poppy seed oil for his oil paintings because it dried quicker. It was obvious to me that he was a great artist and what we would call a genius because he talked in such a way that his whole mental preoccupation was about his paintings and how to arrive at them. He talked to me at great length about the work he was doing and what prompted it. I learnt a lot from him.

Faith O'Reilly (Gibbon), born 1940.

Bright lively man

I first met Stanley in about 1955, so I knew him in my later teenage years. He shopped at Mr Swattons the grocers, opposite our house in Cookham Rise. He was a bit like a little elf really; birdlike, intensely sort of bright, lively and a great conversationalist. He had this habit of tucking his arm round the back of his head and peering quizzically over his glasses, also ruffling his hair. He had this very animated, interested and sort of high-pitched voice. Sometimes in the evenings he would pop in to us for his cocoa and get the art books down from our shelf and just chat. I can remember him standing in our hall as he was about to leave, probably at some unearthly hour because he chatted so much, saying 'You've got to learn to draw before you do anything else, drawing is the essential, the bones of the thing.' He was very adamant because I was doing art 'A' level at the time that I needed to learn to draw first.

Carolyn Lucas (Boxer), born 1943.

Very small and untidy

Oh yes he was very, very small, not a figure of a man in any way – he was like a little cock robin I think. Very self assured, quite a bright skin, mucky, very long black overcoat generally. He was a very well spoken man, no accent – but a rather high pitched voice. Very untidy ; filthy old shoes always, I don't think he ever cleaned those, grey hair straying around. He never stopped talking he was a megalomaniac, he would go on for hour after hour after hour until you really wanted to scream. I said to him once 'Stanley, what

Sir Stanley Spencer in 1958. (Photograph by Eileen and Leslie Gibbon.)

do you think is the most important thing in life?' and he said 'Well in my life I know it's me of course. What else could be of more importance than that? I'm the tops and that's all that matters.' He was terribly self-opinionated, but in many ways he'd got a lot of humility. He really...he was a gem of ordinariness.

Mary Compton

Very talkative

My mother had known him before the war and then, after the war when we came back to Cookham, he used to come for dinner quite a lot. He was very talkative, in fact he never stopped talking and was always extremely pleasant. He was very small and very shabbily dressed, but always quite clean; he wasn't dirty in any way, as people have liked to make out. Let's say, his shirt was worn but it was clean.

Esilda Mezulianik (Castellanos) born 1929.

Sketching father

He was so glad to go out to lunch and he was a great talker so the lunch would be flying all over the table, because he was getting so excited about what he was talking about. He went to lunch with my brother and his wife and afterwards when Peter their son was put up to bed for a rest he went up and sketched him. He sketched my father in 1932, when he was sketching lots of the people in the village, and they all appear in different pictures that he did. My father was the baker and started work very early, three or four o'clock in the morning, and at about ten o'clock he would come in and he would sit in the leather armchair (because of all the flour and stuff) and that day Stanley came in and sketched him – didn't ask or anything just

The Francis Bakery today.

came in. My father was just dropping off to sleep I think by the look of the sketch. He took about twenty-five minutes.

Kate Swan, born 1911.

Sketching mother

My mother's maiden name was Worster, like the road in Cookham Rise. Her family knew the Spencer family very well and she was friendly with Stanley. Mother went to finishing school in Folkstone when she was about fourteen, and while she was there Stanley sent her some sketches. I used to watch Stanley painting, and he would come round to the house. In the early thirties he made a sketch of me and my mother and I would sit and watch him.

Peter Remington, born 1922.

Next-door neighbour

I knew Stanley Spencer because we moved in next door to him, when he lived in Cliveden View, Cookham Rise, in 1952. His grandfather had built that house and he always said 'the house my Grandpappy built is the house I really am most happy in.' He did his work up in that first bedroom, because he said the light was better for his painting. He didn't have an inside lav or a bathroom, he would wash downstairs in the kitchen. Later he had a bathroom put on. Mrs Price, who did for him in the house, lived in the first cottage opposite in High Road and her husband did the garden for him. She used to wash his tweed suits and hang them on the line dripping! She also came across and left meals for him in the kitchen. She would say to him 'have you washed yourself ?'

Pam Giordani, born 1920.

Cliveden View

I used to go up and visit him a lot in Cliveden View. Sometimes he'd be sitting at the piano playing Bach as a break from his painting. I'd sit on the end of the bed in the room he painted in, he never bothered about studios or north light. His bedroom was quite small, big mantle mirror, fireplace, bed with a chair beside it often with a glass of milk and a bit of bread and cheese on it, and then this vast canvas of Christ Preaching at the Cookham Regatta which was unfurled gradually as he worked on it. He chatted to me while he painted, I particularly recall him painting each blade of grass and each check on the ferryman's jacket while I was there. I wouldn't say at the time that I knew him that he was very poor but he certainly lived frugally; Cliveden View was very humbly furnished and he ate next to nothing, and we were always very worried about the fact that he probably only ate properly when he was invited out.

Carolyn Lucas (Boxer), born 1943.

Fernlea

He moved back down to Fernlea in the late fifties. He used one of the rooms above as a kind of bedroom studio. The canvas was unrolled from the wall at Cliveden View and rolled across the room at Fernlea so he could continue with that painting there (Christ Preaching at the Cookham Regatta). That's very clear in my mind because some friends of his had to build some kind of scaffolding so that he could work on the painting. It was a bit higher than the wall in the other place and he had to get up on this scaffolding and work on it there.

Faith O'Reilly (Gibbon), born 1940.

Painting in the churchyard

You'd see him in the churchyard painting and he was only too glad to put down his brush and tell you at great length which part of the bible stories he was depicting. He'd go all through it and it didn't mean a thing to me, but I thought what a marvellous memory.

Sonia Redway, born 1927.

The old iron fence

One day I was on the bus going into Maidenhead and Stanley got on. We were sitting together and he went into rhapsodies about this rusty corrugated iron fence that ran along one side of the road. He said you could see it leading up to God, he saw God in

Stanley Spencer used the angel in Holy Trinity churchyard as a subject in 1935.

everything. To me it was a ghastly, rusty, corrugated iron fence.

Esilda Mezulianik (Castellanos), born 1929.

Not for childrens' ears

As children at Holy Trinity school in the 1930s we used to see Stanley around. He would often be painting on Cookham Moor and we would stand and watch. Sometimes he would chat and sometimes he would just grunt and then we would run away. I knew I'd be in dead trouble if my mother knew that I was standing looking at him. Whenever he was talked about at home I was excluded – it was not for children's ears. I don't think my parents had seen any of his paintings.

Lynda Whitworth (Pat Thompson), born 1925.

The brush-off

As boys we would walk to school and come across Stanley Spencer painting in various places. We would stand and watch him - we would get closer and closer and closer and when we got too close he would flick his paintbrushes at us. He wanted to be left alone while he did his painting. We used to take the mickey out of him and laugh because he was so untidy. He sketched a friend of ours, Bill Clark.

Keith and Barry Hatch, born 1932 and 1935.

Just a villager

He was a dirty old man in an old coat. We used to run after him going 'na na nanana!' Then we used to get fed up with it. Nobody really wanted to know him until he had a knighthood. He was just a person in the village.

Doreen Tubb (Harris), born 1926.

Frightening

As children we were all aware of Stanley Spencer, but I don't think we thought of him as anybody famous. He was quite a frightening person I always felt – wild looking and very scruffy. He certainly was not friendly to children.

Enid Grant (Jenkins), born 1943.

Sculpting Stanley

Stanley was a wonderful talker. He never stopped talking, that was the trouble when I was doing the bust of him. He would come up the stairs of our flat in the afternoon complaining bitterly that he should be painting. When he sat for me he used to sing Gilbert and Sullivan – 'when you're lying awake with a dismal headache….' – and he'd go on from beginning to end. I'd say 'I want to do your mouth now Stanley' so he'd purse his

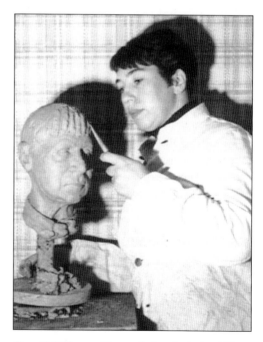

Reca McGibbon working on the bust in the late '50s.

lips up in an unaccustomed look that wasn't Stanley and I had to wait for him to relax, by which time he was off again. He would just talk and talk, often most amusing stories.

Reca McGibbon, born 1915.

Patricia and Dorothy

I met Patricia Preece when I was a schoolgirl, at the bus stop, she used to take the bus once a week. She said to me one day, 'do you think your mother would let me paint you?' I must have been about twelve at the time. I sat, that time, in the living room, everything was shrouded in dustsheets, and that was the only time Patricia painted me. I got a box of sweets for it. I quite liked Patricia, she was tall and thin and when dressed up very elegant, but if you called unexpectedly she used to look terrible. Then time ticked on and after I had left school Dorothy [Hepworth] wanted a model badly. I sat for seventeen [paintings] at different times, they'd take perhaps a month and that was really hard work. It was four days a week from ten o'clock until one o'clock with few breaks. It was a terrible strain because she liked you with your arm on your waist akimbo and twisted round with your legs crossed. Well, cramp, did I get it! At least one got into the Academy in 1947. I didn't think it was one of her best at all. It was called 'Anna with a Rose'. The point was I was never shown any of them and they were all signed Patricia Preece.

Sonia Redway, born 1927.

Stanley and Patricia

One of my memories of Stanley Spencer is grandfather rushing into the bar (of the Gate Hotel where he was publican) saying that Stanley and Patricia were just coming up the Pound, 'come and have a look at her'. I was too young to realise but they were really anti Stanley because they didn't understand his behaviour. They disapproved of the scandal. We all rushed to the window to see Patricia with Stanley. I can see Patricia now, she had a lovely big hat on and a bluey-pink chiffon dress with epaulette sleeves, a fitting bodice and a biased cut skirt in gauze. She looked really very elegant.

Lynda Whitworth (Pat Thompson), born 1925.

The marriage

I remember him most between the years of 1932 and 1937, with us living opposite to him, the break up of his marriage and so forth. I remember seeing Stanley and Patricia Preece so well when they came back from the registry office after being married and the two women and Stanley walking up and down on the Causeway, talking and talking. Of course we didn't know what they were talking about. Nobody knew anything about lesbians in those days but it was a very odd situation altogether. Patricia Preece and Dorothy Hepworth had lived in the village for some long years before all this happened you know. I remember them coming into our shop and talking to my mother. Before they bought the house they lived first in School Lane. I always remember Patricia because she was one of the first to wear the new fashion of coloured pyjama type trousers for women (for being on the river). I remember seeing her dressed in a pair of these made out of pretty material.

Kate Swan, born 1911.

Diamonds and pearls

I worked at Biggs the Jewellers in Maidenhead and sometimes when I walked through the shop there would be Stanley Spencer at the jewellery counter, this Pat (Patricia Preece) at the side of him. They would be showing him diamonds and pearls and she would be picking a piece of jewellery. I did all the accounts at Biggs and that Pat, she'd have a piece of jewellery for about a year and then she'd bring it back and get the full credit and choose another piece. But to see him in this beautiful jewellers in his shabby old coat...

Frances Harvey, born 1918.

Shocking

Stanley told me that Patricia had these rather erotic drawings he'd done that she'd got hold of. She was holding this fact over him and virtually blackmailing him for money. He was scared that Munnings would get hold of them and he would be clapped in prison. In those days it was considered pornographic to paint those kinds of things.

Reca McGibbon, born 1915.

Intimate conversations

When he came to dinner at our house he spoke very much about his marriage to Patricia Preece. In those days you didn't talk openly about lesbianism, but he did. He said he found out Patricia Preece and Dorothy Hepworth were lesbians and talked about the wedding night and booking up at St Ives. It was just a matter of ordinary conversation, and sometimes my mother had other people in, because other people were very anxious to meet him, and this didn't quell him at all, total strangers there. Sometimes he would ring my mother if he was coming to us and say 'Patricia's very down, can I bring her up?' and he used to have a taxi to bring Patricia up. He treated her as if she was something precious, all the time fussing round her. She was a very disagreeable woman. If you spoke directly to her she would answer you but she would never

join directly in the conversation, she was extremely grumpy. She came here about three or four times but if I saw her in the village she would cut me dead, as if I didn't exist. She didn't want to be bothered.

Esilda Mezulianik (Castellanos), born 1929.

Looking after Patricia

Patricia was a very sick woman, she looked ill, she looked absolutely grey and thin. In fact once I put my fingers round the top of her arm and they met, her arms were so thin. Being at Moor Hall (in the 1940s) we were very well fed and I was able to get hold of liver. I used to save it and take it to Patricia and she used to swap her sweet coupons for it. She was too weak to hold a brush. She often met Stanley and they went to Poppets, a little café in the High Street run by the Metz, for lunch. She would walk up the street, near the wall and hold on to the wall, she was so weak. In 1947 the floods were up really badly. Stanley used to come along to Moor Thatch, in his yellow souwester hat, with his pram with coal and provisions because Patricia and Dorothy couldn't get out. Moor Hall and up to School Lane was cut off by the water, everything had to be brought over by punt, the gardeners couldn't do their work so they became the boatmen. Stanley used to come along and wave his arm until they came to collect him. They'd put him and the pram in the boat and take him to Moor Thatch. The water was in the house and they were living upstairs.

Reca McGibbon, born 1915.

Hilda

He used to complain about Patricia a lot. He wasn't terribly un-gentlemanly, but he would say that she was someone who hadn't given the love that he wanted. He talked about

The dedication of Cookham War Memorial, 1919.

Hilda much more, he was writing letters to Hilda at the time that I knew him, who of course was dead, and he didn't hide that. He had explained to me that Hilda had been a spiritualist and that he believed that she could probably still understand these letters. I think he knew, anyway that those letters would be kept and that they would be read by other people and that they would express all the sadness and misery that he felt about the whole affair.

Faith O'Reilly (Gibbon), born 1940.

The war memorial

At the dedication of the War Memorial the local school children (I was at Holy Trinity school) were asked to take flowers and, as the vicar called out the names that were to be remembered, we went up and placed flowers on the memorial for that person. Stanley painted a picture and has put us right by the memorial, whereas I always remember such a long walk to take those flowers up. He stood there and I'm sure he had on a floppy sort of hat as he was standing by the wall sketching. We all had these little panama hats that school children wore, but in the picture he has painted us with large floppy hats; but he has got my ringlets coming down the side.

Kate Swan, born 1911.

Daphne Charlton

I knew Daphne Charlton. She used to come and stay with Stanley and he would ring up my mother and say 'Daphne's coming, I can't work when she's here' – because Daphne was a very overpowering lady – 'could she stay with you?' My mother used to say yes because we had the room and Daphne used to land on us. She was very Amazonian, very tall and large without being fat. Daphne gave a party at Cliveden View when she was there and would ask my mother for flowers, so I as a seventeen-year-old would be sent down with a basket laden with flowers. Stanley was very much the lion of a party, he was used to being the centre of attention.

Esilda Mezulianik (Castellanos), born 1929.

The Maurice Collis book

I knew nothing about Stanley's private life until the furore over Maurice Collis' book, and I remember that very clearly because everybody in the village was up in arms – people deeply resented this portrait of him.

Carolyn Lucas (Boxer), born 1943.

Cookham Arts Club

I was in the Cookham Arts Club for 1954 and it was soon after that that we invited him along. We had yearly art exhibitions and Stanley used to send pictures along, mostly he lent them but some of them were for sale,

at vastly different prices from today! I've still got a letter from when I insured some of his pictures in 1959 or 1960 and the total insurance bill was £5. There were some quite well known ones in there; there were two drawings of Jack Martineau, and the Swiss child and the paintings. He came and gave quite a good demonstration, he was very sound on things like that. Some of us were only learning to paint really and he gave a lot of very good tips. He was always willing to talk and to be helpful in that way, he wasn't at all niggledy about giving advice.

Mary Compton.

His vision

Stanley told me this story. He felt as if he was hanging onto Cookham Bridge, in the middle, and the other leading artists of the day were hanging onto him, dangling down below him. It was absolutely vital that he hung onto

A Cookham Arts Club meeting.

Cookham Bridge for dear life and his ideas about painting or they'd all go down into the river and be drowned. He had to hold them all together. This happened at a time when he felt he was a forgotten artist and that all the limelight, news and publicity had gone to the likes of Henry Moore, John Piper, Graham Sutherland, Paul Nash and others. He felt that something vital that he'd seen was being lost and forgotten. That hurt him personally. It is interesting to see how his mind worked; he images this as if it is a painting.

Ralph Thompson, born 1913.

'St Francis and the Birds'

'St Francis and the Birds' was quite a painting. I asked him about it one day and he said 'You see that tap (in the kitchen), I suddenly saw that tap one morning and I thought that's a good shape, I think I'll use that shape for the head of St Francis'. If you look at the painting, there it is, a sort of tap head.

Faith O'Reilly (Gibbon), born 1940.

'The Crucifixion'

At the time of the 1958 exhibition he had just painted 'The Crucifixion'. I was just looking at it and old Stanley came along and dug me in the ribs and said 'I've got you in at last'. He said 'That's you with the nails in your mouth nailing up the cross'. I am a carpenter by trade.

Eddie Smyth, born 1909.

Mains drainage

I remember seeing 'The Crucifixion' in various stages. I remember it arising out of putting in mains drainage in Cookham. We

Cookham Bridge in 1925.

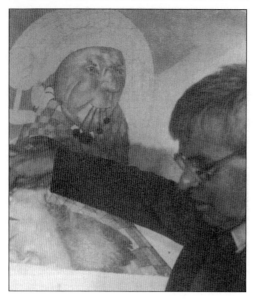

Spencer with his painting, 'The Crucifixion'.
(Photograph by Eileen and Leslie Gibbon)

had workmen in the village for months and months digging up the drains. The picture shows the rubble from the drainage work.

Carolyn Lucas (Boxer), born 1943.

Helping hand

I helped him with some of the painting at the bottom of 'The Crucifixion'. He had to get it finished and he wasn't very well. He was telling me exactly what to do, saying 'mix that colour exactly' so there are little patches of painting that I helped with. When he was painting Christ preaching at Cookham Regatta he said to me, 'what colour do you think I should put on this dress, what colour should I use here?'

Faith O'Reilly (Gibbon), born 1940.

Naughty boy fun

Stanley was a very chirpy, lively, wonderful

character to be with. I met him mid-war when he was doing the Glasgow paintings. I remember him with his lavatory paper sketches and recall the childish glee, a real sort of glee, naughty boy fun, with which he produced these. He'd already got the canvases, I went to his studio at the end of the garden in Cookham where he was working on the riveters and welders. He did studies up in Scotland but his imagination was the dominant factor.

Ralph Thomspon, born 1913.

Pretty masterly

On the commissioned portraits he would work fairly slowly. His method of painting was one that was not usual at the time, that was that you made no mistakes, in other words you mixed up the right colour and you put it on the first time. That seemed to be mainly the way he was able to work. He did scrape off very occasionally, but most of the time he would look at the palette, mix the right colour and put it on and it would be right pretty masterly.

Faith O'Reilly (Gibbon), born 1940.

Raising Church funds

In 1958 we were raising money to buy Church House (Park House it was called then) along the Maidenhead Road. Stanley came up with an idea to have a little exhibition to raise £50. The exhibition ran for three weeks and we made £4,500! It was during Trinity week. All the religious paintings were in the church and the others were in the Vicarage. The Westropps were a super couple, they gave their whole house up to it: all up the stairs, all the landings, all downstairs. People were in and out of the house all the time. We used a summer house as a box office. They paid to go into the vicarage, but the church was free, or donations to the collection. It was really good fun. They auctioned off the painting he was doing in the churchyard and it was sold for £345, I think. The first Wednesday he gave a talk in the church, the church was fairly full – the two following Wednesdays the church was packed and he talked from half past ten to one o'clock in the morning, continually. Something different every time, and he's walking round the church all the time talking about the various paintings in the church, explaining it all. Stanley was well away! The BBC weren't interested at all at first, but ITV came down. Monday came, and the BBC were clamouring to come in.

Eddie Smyth, born 1909.

With Alf Boxer on the Vicarage lawn in 1958.

Didn't need a microphone

Stanley did a talk at the 1958 exhibition. It was packed, Lord Astor, the Mayor and other local notabilities came. He spoke extremely well. He needed no mike, he had a beautifully produced, rather high pitched speaking voice, he didn't have to raise it, it was so well placed you could hear every word. He had a lot of personal charm, I found him fascinating, I was really enthralled.

Sonia Redway, born 1927.

1958 exhibition

My father Alfred Boxer was involved in organising the 1958 Exhibition. He was an advertising manager so he knew a lot about publicity and he took responsibility for press and publicity. He designed all the catalogues and written material and press releases. I can remember shepherding people around the Exhibition.

Carolyn Lucas (Boxer), born 1943.

Love of music

When I had known him a little bit I asked him if he would come up to my house. He was then living at Annie's house in Cookham Rise (Cliveden View) so he just had to climb the hill, it was a lovely old walk and he used to come up to tea, for dripping toast. Remember the time of course, it was when food was scarce and pork dripping was very tasty! One felt he was part of the family within ten minutes, he was so easy, so there in the living of the minute. One of the attractions was our piano and he would sit down and play Bach, no score, no music, he would stop and fumble a bit and then play on, but we were all astonished at the relationship with Stanley and this piano and the feeling for the music that came out of it.

Ralph Thompson, born 1913.

Composing

When I asked him what gave him the idea for that fantastic composition [the end wall of the Burghclere Chapel] he explained that it was a bit like a Bach fugue. He then demonstrated on the piano how the fugue goes, in the sense that you start with a small series of notes and then you build it bigger and bigger and bigger. So if you look at the painting, it is musical in that sense; the crosses are all coming down from bigger to smaller or smaller to bigger and it's like a kind of symbol that is used in that way. In the same way as a composer might use three notes on the piano, in different series and contexts and registers. So I could see the relationship between that and the music.

Faith O'Reilly (Gibbon), born 1940.

Illness

As we got to know him better Stanley would come next door to us for supper, in his pyjamas with his outside trousers on top and we used to get on very well, he was very easy, very nice. He came in one Christmas Eve and

Bust of Sir Stanley Spencer by Reca McGibbon.

had supper with us and later that night my son, whose bedroom was on Stanley's side of the house, kept saying he could hear someone shouting. I never thought any thing much about it, but later I woke and I could hear Stanley shouting for my husband who was a doctor. My husband Ennis spent Christmas Day there and later the GP Bill Edwards went round. That was the start of his last long nasty illness.

Pam Giordani, born 1920.

Duets

In 1958 when Stanley was a very sick man he used to come up to the house. He was crazy about Bach and he used to sit at the piano and play with one hand and my husband, Paul, would fill in all the rest. He was in such pain he found it hard to sit. Francis Ffrancon Davis was also around, they used to play duets and Stanley loved it, he loved music.

Esilda Mezulianik (Castellanos), born 1929.

Last Days

I watched the painting of that final self-portrait. It was actually set in the hallway of Fernlea, but of course he was doing it in the mirror. He used some kind of patterning on the paper behind him that was in the hallway. The work he did was highly concentrated and it wasn't just whacking a bit of light and dark on, it was highly observed, the eyes behind the glasses and so on. It was painful to watch him going through that. I think I must have visited him every couple of days, it took about a week. When he went into hospital I went over to see him and asked him what he wanted. He said he'd like a little book about Brueghel, so I took him a little book about Brueghel and that was the last time I saw him.

Faith O'Reilly (Gibbon), born 1940.